Careers in Focus

GOVERNMENT

SECOND EDITION

Ferguson
An imprint of Infobase Publishing

Careers in Focus: Government, Second Edition

Ferguson
An imprint of Infobase Publishing
132 West 31st Street
New York NY 10001

ISBN-10: 0-8160-6568-3
ISBN-13: 978-0-8160-6568-4

Library of Congress Cataloging-in-Publication Data

Careers in focus. Government.—2nd ed.
    p. cm.
  Includes index.
  ISBN-13: 978-0-8160-6568-4 (hc:alk paper)
  1. United States—Officials and employees—Juvenile literature. 2. Administrative agencies—United States—Officials and employees—Vocational guidance—Juvenile literature. 3. Local officials and employees—United States—Vocational guidance—Juvenile literature. 4. Politics, Practical—United States—Vocational guidance—Juvenile literature.
JK421.C25 2007
351.73023—dc22

2006034081

Text design by David Strelecky
Cover design by Joo Young An

Printed in the United States of America

MP MSRF 10 9 8 7 6 5 4 3 2 1

This book is printed on acid-free paper.

Table of Contents

Introduction............................. 1

Ambassadors 5

City Managers 14

Congressional Aides..................... 22

Customs Officials...................... 31

Deputy U.S. Marshals 40

FBI Agents 48

Federal and State Officials 60

Federal Aviation Security Workers 69

Fish and Game Wardens.................. 76

Foreign Service Officers 83

Health and Regulatory Inspectors 93

Intelligence Officers 105

Interpreters and Translators............. 114

Judges................................. 125

Mail Carriers 133

Military Workers 142

National Park Service Employees 153

Regional and Local Officials 165

Secret Service Special Agents 174

Urban and Regional Planners............. 185

Index................................. 195

Introduction

Careers in Focus: Government describes a variety of careers in local, state, and federal government—in city councils, legislatures, foreign consulates, national parks, airports, factories, offices, courtrooms, and countless other settings. These careers are as diverse in nature as they are in their earnings and educational requirements.

Opportunities are available for those interested in public service (appointed and elected officials); protecting their fellow citizens from crime, including terrorism (airport security workers, deputy U.S. marshals, FBI Agents, intelligence officers, and Secret Service Special Agents); serving in the military; protecting the environment (fish and game wardens, National Park Service workers); working in diplomatic relations (ambassadors, Foreign Service officers, interpreters, and translators); playing a key role in the legal system (judges); and working in support positions that are integral to keeping our government running smoothly and efficiently (clerks, computer specialists, congressional aides, and other professionals).

Earnings in government range from less than $16,000 for beginning soldiers to $400,000 for the president of the United States.

Careers in government are available to those with a wide variety of educational backgrounds. For example, customs officials and mail carriers require only a high school diploma. Other government careers require some postsecondary training (airport security workers) or a bachelor's degree (city managers, FBI Agents, Foreign Service officers, interpreters, and translators, National Park Service workers, and urban and regional planners). Federal and state judges are usually required to have a law degree; approximately 40 states allow those with a bachelor's degree and work experience to hold limited-jurisdiction judgeships.

Overall, the federal government, excluding the U.S. Postal Service, employed approximately 1.9 million civilian workers in 2004. Fewer than 17 percent worked in the Washington, D.C. area, and 5 percent worked overseas. Approximately 7.9 million people were employed by state and local governments (excluding education and hospitals) in 2004. Seventy percent of this total were employed by local government.

The U.S. Department of Labor predicts that employment in state and local government will grow by 11 percent through 2014. Employment at the federal level is expected to grow by 2.5 percent through 2014. Although growth at all government levels is expected to be slower than the average for all industries, opportunities will be available to applicants with advanced educational training and or specialized skills and training.

Each article in this book discusses a particular government career in detail. The articles in *Careers in Focus: Government* appear in Ferguson's *Encyclopedia of Careers and Vocational Guidance* but have been updated and revised with the latest information from the U.S. Department of Labor, professional organizations, and other sources. The following paragraphs detail the sections and features that appear in the book.

The **Quick Facts** section provides a brief summary of the career including recommended school subjects, personal skills, work environment, minimum educational requirements, salary ranges, certification or licensing requirements, and employment outlook. This section also provides acronyms and identification numbers for the following government classification indexes: the Dictionary of Occupational Titles (DOT), the Guide to Occupational Exploration (GOE), the National Occupational Classification (NOC) Index, and the Occupational Information Network (O*NET)-Standard Occupational Classification System (SOC) index. The DOT, GOE, and O*NET-SOC indexes have been created by the U.S. government; the NOC index is Canada's career classification system. Readers can use the identification numbers listed in the Quick Facts section to access further information about a career. Print editions of the DOT (*Dictionary of Occupational Titles*. Indianapolis, Ind.: JIST Works, 1991) and GOE (*The Complete Guide for Occupational Exploration*. Indianapolis, Ind.: JIST Works, 1993) are available at libraries. Electronic versions of the NOC (http://www23.hrdc-drhc. gc.ca) and O*NET-SOC (http://online.onetcenter.org) are available on the Internet. When no DOT, GOE, NOC, or O*NET-SOC numbers are present, this means that the U.S. Department of Labor or Human Resources Development Canada has not created a numerical designation for this career. In this instance, you will see the acronym "N/A" or not available.

The **Overview** section is a brief introductory description of the duties and responsibilities involved in this career. Oftentimes, a career may have a variety of job titles. When this is the case, alternative career titles are presented. The **History** section describes the history of the particular job as it relates to the overall development of its industry or field. **The Job** describes the primary and secondary duties of the job. **Requirements** discusses high school and post-secondary education and training requirements, any certification or licensing that is necessary, and other personal requirements for success in the job. **Exploring** offers suggestions on how to gain experience in or knowledge of the particular job before making a firm educational and financial commitment. The focus is on what can be done while still in high school (or in the early years of college) to gain a better understanding of the job. The **Employers** section gives an overview of typical places of employment for the job. **Starting Out** discusses the best ways to land that first job, be it through the college placement office, newspaper ads, or personal contact. The **Advancement** section describes what kind of career path to expect from the job and how to get there. **Earnings** lists salary ranges and describes the typical fringe benefits. The **Work Environment** section describes the typical surroundings and conditions of employment—whether indoors or outdoors, noisy or quiet, social or independent. Also discussed are typical hours worked, any seasonal fluctuations, and the stresses and strains of the job. The **Outlook** section summarizes the job in terms of the general economy and industry projections. For the most part, Outlook information is obtained from the U.S. Bureau of Labor Statistics and is supplemented by information taken from professional associations. Job growth terms follow those used in the *Occupational Outlook Handbook*. Growth described as "much faster than the average" means an increase of 27 percent or more. Growth described as "faster than the average" means an increase of 18 to 26 percent. Growth described as "about as fast as the average" means an increase of 9 to 17 percent. Growth described as "more slowly than the average" means an increase of 0 to 8 percent. "Decline" means a decrease by any amount. Each article ends with **For More Information,** which lists organizations that provide information on training, education, internships, scholarships, and job placement.

Careers in Focus: Government also includes photos, informative sidebars, and interviews with professionals in the field.

Ambassadors

OVERVIEW

Ambassadors manage the operations of the U.S. embassies in other countries. An embassy is the headquarters of a U.S. diplomatic mission established in the capital city of a foreign country. According to the U.S. Department of State, the United States maintains diplomatic relations with nearly 180 of the other 190 U.N. members (plus the Vatican in Rome) and has an embassy in most foreign capitals. Each embassy is headed by only one ambassador. Charged with the responsibility of maintaining diplomatic relations, an ambassador represents the president in matters of foreign policy. Ambassadors help to promote peace, trade, and the exchange of information between the United States and foreign lands.

HISTORY

Even in the earliest years of the United States, diplomacy was recognized as an important element of a strong government. Men such as Benjamin Franklin, John Adams, John Jay, and Francis Dana were chosen for their intelligence, strength of character, and powers of persuasion to enlist the support of foreign countries for American independence. Benjamin Franklin was so successful in his commission to France that he inspired a pre-Disney marketing blitz—the French put his picture on watches, jewelry, and even snuffboxes. And the women of France had their hair done to resemble the fur caps Franklin wore. However, not all diplomats

QUICK FACTS

School Subjects
Foreign language
Government

Personal Skills
Communication/ideas
Leadership/management

Work Environment
Primarily indoors
Primarily multiple
  locations

Minimum Education Level
Bachelor's degree

Salary Range
$100,000 to $118,000 to
  $125,000

Certification or Licensing
None available

Outlook
Little change or more slowly
  than the average

DOT
188

GOE
11.09.03

NOC
4168

O*NET-SOC
N/A

enjoyed such stardom; Francis Dana spent a cold, unproductive two years in Russia, unable to speak the language and incapable of convincing Catherine II to support American independence.

Established in 1789, the State Department was placed under the direction of Thomas Jefferson, the first U.S. secretary of state and the senior member of President Washington's cabinet. It was his responsibility to initiate foreign policy on behalf of the U.S. government, advise the president on matters related to foreign policy, and administer the foreign affairs of the United States with the help of employees both at home and abroad.

Before the invention of radio, telegraph, telephone, and e-mail, the ambassador was entrusted to make final, binding decisions on behalf of the United States. More immediate means of communication narrowed the distances between embassies and their home countries; though today's ambassadors represent the president and actively contribute to international relations, they are more restricted in their powers.

THE JOB

Iceland. New Zealand. Venezuela. Sweden. Jordan. Egypt. Ambassadors to these or one of the nearly 180 countries that host U.S. embassies in their capital cities coordinate the operations of hundreds of government officers. An embassy serves as the headquarters for Foreign Service Officers (FSOs) and other personnel, all working together to maintain a positive, productive relationship between the host country and the United States. Though the work is important, the post of ambassador is sometimes largely ceremonial. The president offers an ambassadorship to someone who has a long, dignified history of political service or to a wealthy supporter of the president's political party. An ambassador will stay at a post for two to six years. *Career ambassadors* are Foreign Service officers; *noncareer ambassadors* are outside of the Foreign Service.

Ambassadors address many different concerns, such as security, trade, tourism, environmental protection, and health care. They are involved in establishing and maintaining international agreements, such as nuclear test bans and ozone-layer protection. They help to promote peace and stability and open new markets. When negotiating treaties and introducing policies, they help the people of the host country understand the U.S. position, while also helping the United States understand the host country's position.

Ambassadors spend much of their time meeting government officials and private citizens of the host country. Together they identify subjects of mutual interest, such as medical research and the development of new technologies. They meet those involved in private industry in the country, including Americans doing business there. When a country is struggling as a result of natural disasters, epidemics, and other problems, ambassadors may pursue aid from the United States.

Ambassadors' work isn't limited to the city in which the embassy is located. They travel across the country to learn about the other cities and regions and to meet the cities' representatives. Among the people of the country, ambassadors promote a good attitude toward the United States, as well as travel, business, and educational opportunities. When important U.S. visitors such as the president, first lady, and secretary of state arrive in the country, the ambassador serves as host, introducing them to the country and its officials.

Of course, ambassadors for different countries must address very different issues, such as environmental concerns, the state of education and health care, political structure, agriculture, and industry. For example, the United States has entered agreements with Budapest, Hungary; Bangkok, Thailand; and Gabarone, Botswana; to establish International Law Enforcement Academies. The academies, jointly financed, managed, and staffed by the cooperating nations, initially provide training to police and government officials.

REQUIREMENTS

High School

In order to pursue any work that involves foreign government, you need a well-rounded education. Talk to your guidance counselor about classes that will be most helpful in preparing for college. Courses in American history, western civilization, government, and world history are important, as well as classes in math and economics. English composition will help you develop writing and communication skills. Any foreign language course will give you a good foundation in language study—many ambassadors know more than two languages. Journalism courses develop writing and editing skills and keep you informed about current events.

Postsecondary Training

Many ambassadors and FSOs hold master's degrees and doctorates in international relations, political science, or economics. Many also hold law degrees. As an undergraduate, you
should take general-requirement courses in English literature,
foreign language, composition, geography, and statistics, along
with courses for your particular major. There are many undergraduate majors relevant to foreign service, including foreign
language, economics, political science, journalism, education,
business, and English. You may also want to consider programs
designed specifically for foreign service and international relations. The Georgetown University Edmund A. Walsh School
of Foreign Service (http://www.georgetown.edu/sfs) has undergraduate and graduate programs designed to prepare students
for careers in international affairs. Many luminaries have graduated from the school, including Bill Clinton in 1968; former
Secretary of State Madeleine Albright has served as a member
of the school's faculty. Postgraduate programs, especially those
in political science, are also very useful.

"Career Ambassador" is the highest rank for senior officers
of the Foreign Service, but you don't have to be an FSO to be an
ambassador. If you do choose to pursue work as an officer, the
Foreign Service offers internship opportunities to college students in their junior and senior years and to graduate students.
About half of these unpaid internships are based in Washington,
D.C., while the other half are at U.S. embassies and consulates
overseas. Interns may write reports, assist with trade negotiations, work with budget projects, or process visas or passports.
The Foreign Service also offers a Foreign Affairs Fellowship Program, which provides funding to undergraduate and graduate
students preparing academically to enter the Foreign Service.

Other Requirements

Ambassadors are usually already successful in their careers before
being nominated for an ambassadorship. They also have some
connection to top officials in the U.S. government. To achieve
such success and good connections, you must be very intelligent
and knowledgeable about government and politics. It is important
to earn good grades, so as to earn admission to top schools, where
such connections can be made. You should be comfortable in a
leadership role and extremely ambitious and motivated—those
who serve as ambassadors have often achieved success in a num-

ber of different areas and have held a variety of powerful positions. Also, you should be flexible and adaptable to new cultures and traditions. You must be interested in the histories of foreign cultures and respectful of the practices of other nations. People skills are important for dealing diplomatically with officials from other countries.

EXPLORING

As a member of a foreign language club at your school, you may have the opportunity to visit other countries. If such programs don't exist, check with your guidance counselor or school librarian about discounted foreign travel packages available to student groups. Also ask them about student exchange programs, if you're interested in spending several weeks in another country. There's also a People to People Student Ambassador Program, which offers summer travel opportunities to students in grades six through 12. To learn about the expenses, destinations, and the application process, visit http://www.studentambassadors.org. Visit the Department of State Web site (http://www.state.gov) to read the biographies of ambassadors around the world and for links to individual embassy Web sites.

The American Foreign Service Association (AFSA), a professional association serving FSOs, publishes the *Foreign Service Journal* (http://www.afsa.org/fsj), which features articles by FSOs and academics that can give you insight into the Foreign Service. AFSA offers a discount on student subscriptions.

EMPLOYERS

Ambassadors work for the U.S. State Department. They represent the interests of the president through the secretary of state. Many ambassadors are FSOs who have worked up through the ranks of the Foreign Service.

STARTING OUT

Those appointed as ambassadors have already succeeded in their individual careers. While many ambassadors have worked in the Foreign Service in some capacity, many others have established themselves in other ways. They have worked as directors in other government agencies and as members of the U.S. Congress. They

Zalmay Khalilzad, the U.S. ambassador to Iraq, conducts a press conference at the Pentagon. *(U.S. Department of Defense)*

have served on the faculty of colleges and universities. They have directed philanthropic organizations and run large companies. Before getting an ambassadorship, ambassadors may have already had a great deal of experience with a particular country, possibly having served as *deputy chief of mission* (the second in command of an embassy). Or they may have been involved in negotiating international agreements or in establishing new markets for the country.

ADVANCEMENT

After being nominated for an ambassadorship by the president, nominees are then confirmed by the Senate. Positions with the Foreign Service are rotational, so the length of an ambassador's term varies. Most ambassadors serve only a few years with an embassy. After leaving a post, they may go on to serve as ambassador at a U.S. embassy in another country. Some career ambassadors spend several years moving from embassy to embassy. Many ambassadors have published books on foreign policy, international affairs, and world trade.

EARNINGS

Ambassadors earn salaries that range from $100,000 to $125,000, according to the State Department. FSOs receive health benefits, life insurance, and retirement benefits that include a pension plan.

WORK ENVIRONMENT

Ambassadors are highly respected. They may have the opportunity to live in comfortable quarters in glamorous cities or may be living in nations wracked by poverty and political unrest. Regardless of the area of the world, ambassadors have the chance to learn about a culture from the inside. Working alongside a nation's government officials, they are exposed to the art, food, industry, politics, and language of another country while meeting some of the country's most interesting and notable figures. They also have the opportunity to play host to visiting dignitaries from the United States.

Most embassy offices overseas are clean, pleasant, and well equipped, but ambassadors may occasionally travel into areas that present health hazards. Customs may differ considerably, medical care may be substandard or nonexistent, the climate may be extreme, or other hardships may exist. In some countries, there is the danger of earthquakes, typhoons, or floods; in others, there is the danger of political upheaval.

Although embassy hours are normally the usual office hours of the host country, other tasks of the job may involve outside activities, such as attending or hosting dinners, lectures, public functions, and other necessary social engagements.

OUTLOOK

Since the end of the Cold War, the responsibilities of ambassadors and Foreign Service officers have increased; war, drug trade, nuclear smuggling, and terrorism are some of the issues confronting embassies today. Those interested in protecting diplomacy and the strength of the Foreign Service need to closely follow relevant legislation, as well as promote the importance of international affairs. Those with the strongest educational backgrounds and experience in the Foreign Service will have the best prospects of landing a coveted position as an ambassador or other professional in the Foreign Service.

FOR MORE INFORMATION

This professional organization serving current and retired Foreign Service Officers has an informative Web site and publishes additional career information. To read selected publications online (including Inside a U.S. Embassy*) or for additional information, contact*
American Foreign Service Association
2101 E Street, NW
Washington, DC 20037-2916
Tel: 800-704-2372
Email: member@afsa.org
http://www.afsa.org

The U.S. Department of State has a wealth of career information on its Web site, along with information about internships, the history of the Foreign Service, and current ambassadors and embassies. To request brochures, contact

U.S. Foreign Service
U.S. Department of State
2401 E Street, NW, Suite 518 H
Washington, DC 20522-0001
Email: Careers@state.gov
http://careers.state.gov

City Managers

School Subjects
Business
Government
Mathematics

Personal Skills
Communication/ideas
Leadership/management

Work Environment
Primarily indoors
Primarily multiple locations

Minimum Education Level
Bachelor's degree

Salary Range
$28,489 to $88,695 to
$137,887

Certification or Licensing
None available

Outlook
More slowly than the average

DOT
188

GOE
13.01.01

NOC
0414

O*NET-SOC
N/A

OVERVIEW

A *city manager* is an administrator who coordinates the day-to-day running of a local government. Usually an appointed position, the manager directs the administration of city or county government in accordance with the policies determined by the city council or other elected authority.

HISTORY

There have been all sorts of governments and political theories in our world's history, and much of the structure of U.S. government is based on the theories and practices of other nations. The "council-manager" form of government, however, is truly American in origin. With government reforms of the early 1900s came government managers. Before the reform, cities were run by city councils or boards of aldermen. Because of rigged elections and other corruption by aldermen, a mayoral form of government was brought into practice. The council-manager form of government also evolved. Though a mayor is elected and holds political power, the city manager is appointed by the council. When the elected officials develop policies, the city managers use their administrative and management skills to put these policies into action.

Some Southern towns began to develop council-manager forms of government as early as 1908; Dayton, Ohio, became the first large city to put the council-manager form into place in 1913. According to the International City/County Management Association (ICMA), 3,475 cities operate in the council-manager form today. More than 92 million people live in these communities.

THE JOB

Have more bus routes been added to provide transportation to a new shopping area? Has the small park near the lake been cleaned up so children can play safely there? Will a new performing arts center be built downtown? These are some of the kinds of questions a city manager faces on the job. Even the smallest community has hundreds of concerns, from quality daycare options for its citizens to proper housing for the elderly, from maintaining strong law enforcement in the city to preserving the surrounding environment. Every day, local newspapers feature all the changes underway in their communities. The mayor introduces these developments, speaking to reporters and appearing on the TV news and at city meetings. But it's the city manager who works behind the scenes to put these changes into effect. A city manager uses managerial experience and skills to determine what programs are needed in the community, to design the programs, and to implement them. The council-manager form of government is somewhat like a smooth-running business—the executives make the decisions about a company, while the managers see that these decisions are put into practice efficiently and effectively.

A city has many different departments in place to collect and disburse taxes, enforce laws, maintain public health and a ready fire department, construct public works such as parks and other recreational facilities, and purchase supplies and equipment. The city manager prepares budgets of the costs of these services and submits estimates to the elected officials for approval. The manager is also responsible for providing reports of ongoing and completed work and projects to the representatives of the residents. The city manager keeps in touch with the community in order to understand what is most important to the people of the city. A city manager also needs to stay several steps ahead, in order to plan for growth, population expansion, and public services. To oversee planning for population growth, crime prevention, street repairs, law enforcement, and pollution and traffic management problems, the manager prepares proposals and recommends zoning regulations. The manager then presents these proposals at meetings of the elected authorities as well as at public meetings of citizens.

In addition to developing plans and budgets, city managers meet with private groups and individuals who represent special interests. Managers explain programs, policies, and projects. They may also seek to enlist the aid of citizen groups in a variety of projects that help the public as a whole. They work closely with urban planners to coordinate new and existing programs. In smaller cities that have no planning staff, this work may be done entirely by the manager. Additional staff may be provided for the city manager of a large city, including an assistant city manager, department head assistants, administrative assistants, and management analysts.

The staff members of a city manager have a variety of titles and responsibilities. Changes in administration are studied and recommended by *management analysts*. Administrative and staff work, such as compiling statistics and planning work procedures, is done by *administrative assistants,* also called *executive assistants*. Department head assistants may work in several areas, such as law enforcement, finance, or law, but they are generally responsible for just one area. *Assistant city managers* are responsible for specific projects, such as developing the annual budget, as well as organizing and coordinating programs. They may supervise city employees and perform other administrative tasks, such as answering correspondence, receiving visitors, preparing reports, and monitoring programs.

REQUIREMENTS

High School
Take courses in government and social studies to learn about the nature of cities and counties. Math and business courses are important because you'll be working with budgets and statistics and preparing financial reports. English and composition courses and speech and debate teams are also very important, as you'll need good communication skills for presenting your thoughts and ideas to policy makers, special interest groups, and the community. Computer science is an important tool in any administrative profession. Take journalism courses and report for your school newspaper to learn about research and conducting polls and surveys.

Postsecondary Training
You'll need at least a bachelor's degree to work as a city manager. As an undergraduate, you'll major in such programs as public administration, political science, sociology, or business. The ICMA notes that an increasing number of local governments are requiring job candidates for manager positions to have master's degrees in public administration or business. Programs resulting in a master's in public administration (M.P.A) are available all across the country; some schools offer dual degrees, allowing you to also pursue a master's of business administration or master's of social work along with the M.P.A. The National Association of Schools of Public Affairs and Administration (NASPAA) offers voluntary accreditation to schools with degree

programs in public affairs and administration. The association has a membership of approximately 250 schools, of which approximately 135 are accredited. The NASPAA's Web site (http://www.naspaa.org) provides a roster of accredited programs, which is updated annually.

Course work in public administration programs covers topics such as finance, budgeting, municipal law, legal issues, personnel management, and the political aspects of urban problems. Degree requirements in some schools also include completion of an internship program in a city manager's office that may last from six months to a year, during which time the degree candidate observes local government operations and does research under the direct supervision of the city manager.

People planning to enter city management positions frequently must pass civil service examinations. This is one way to become eligible for appointments to local government. Other requirements will vary from place to place. Most positions require knowledge of computerized tax and utility billing, electronic traffic control, and applications of systems analysis to urban problems.

Other Requirements

"You have to have the will, desire, and strength to want to lead an organization," says Michael Roberto, former city manager of Clearwater, Florida. He emphasizes that, as manager, you're the person held primarily responsible for the administration of the city. You should have a thick skin: "You'll be yelled at a lot," he says. In addition to handling the complaints, you must be able to handle the stress of the job and the long and frequently unpredictable hours that are required. "But you're only limited by your dreams in what you can create," Roberto says.

You'll need to be decisive, confident, and staunch in making managerial decisions. You need to be skilled at solving problems, while flexible enough to consider the ideas of others. Managers must also have a knack for working with people, have the ability to negotiate and tactfully debate with coworkers and other officials, and be able to listen to the opinions and concerns of the people they represent.

EXPLORING

You can learn about public administration by becoming involved in student government or by serving as an officer for a school club, such as a business or Internet club. A summer job in a local government

Forms of Government, 2005

Council-Manager	3,475	48.8 percent
Mayor-Council	3,091	43.4 percent
Town Meeting	338	4.7 percent
Commission	145	2.0 percent
Representative Town Meeting	63	0.8 percent

(Note: Statistics for municipalities with populations of 2,500 or greater)

Source: International City/County Management Association

office can give you a lot of insight into the workings of a city. Work for the school newspaper and you'll learn about budgets, projects, and school administrators. An internship with a local newspaper or radio or TV station may give you the opportunity to interview the mayor, council members, and the city manager about city administration.

EMPLOYERS

Cities large and small have council-manager forms of government and require city managers for the administration of policies and programs. Counties and suburbs also have managers. The ICMA reports that out of the 237 American cities with more than 100,000 residents, 141 use a council-manager form of government. Those with a master's degree in public administration may find work as a city planner. Other employment possibilities include working as an administrator of a hospital or an association or in private industry. Some professionals with this background work as instructors for undergraduate public administration programs at universities or community colleges.

STARTING OUT

In addition to college internships with local public administrators, you can apply to the ICMA internship programs. There is heavy competition for these internship positions because they often lead to full-time work. The ICMA also publishes a newsletter announcing job vacancies. Nearly all city managers begin as management assistants. As a new graduate, you'll work as a management analyst or administrative assistant to city managers for several years to gain experience in solving urban problems, coordinating public services, and applying management techniques. Or you may work in a specific department such as finance, public works, civil engineering, or planning. You'll acquire supervisory skills and also work as an assistant city manager or department head assistant. After a few years of competent service, you may be hired to manage a community.

Other avenues of potential employment include listings in the job sections of newspapers and professional journals. There are also private firms that specialize in filling government job openings. Those willing to relocate to smaller cities at lower salaries should have better job opportunities.

ADVANCEMENT

An assistant to a city manager is gradually given more responsibilities and assignments as he or she gains experience. At least five years of experience are generally necessary to compete for the position of city manager. City managers are often employed in small cities at first, and during their careers they may seek and obtain appointments in growing cities. Experienced managers may become heads of regional government councils; others may serve several small jurisdictions at one time. Those city managers with a master's degree in business management, political science, urban planning, or law stand the best chance for employment.

EARNINGS

City managers' earnings vary according to such factors as the size of the city, the city's geographical location, and the manager's education and experience. The ICMA reports that in 2004, the mean annual income for city managers ranged from an average of $48,772 per year (in the East-South Central region) to $91,552 (on the Pacific Coast). Overall salaries ranged from a low of approximately $28,489 annually to a high of approximately $137,887 during that same period. According to the International City/County Management Association, city managers had median annual salaries of $88,695 in 2004.

Salaries are set by the city council, and good city managers are sometimes given higher than average pay as an incentive to keep them from seeking more lucrative opportunities. Benefits for city managers include paid vacations, health insurance, sick leave, and retirement plans. Cities may also pay travel and moving expenses and provide a city car or a car allowance.

WORK ENVIRONMENT

Typically a city manager has an office and possibly a trained staff to assist him or her. But a city manager also spends many hours attending meetings. To provide information to citizens on current government operations or to advocate certain programs, the manager frequently appears at public meetings and other civic functions and often visits government departments and inspects work sites. A city manager often works overtime at night and on weekends reading and writing reports or finishing paperwork. The manager also needs to attend dinners and evening events and go out of town for conferences. Any extra days worked on weekends are usually compensated for in vacation time or additional pay. "The long hours," Michael Roberto says, "can be tough on your home life, tough on your family." A city manager can be called at any hour of the day or night in times of crisis. Managers must be prepared for sometimes stressful interaction with coworkers and constituents, as well as the acclaim that comes to them for completing a job successfully or solving a particularly complex problem. "You're scrutinized by the press," Roberto says, and he emphasizes that a manager shouldn't be too affected by the coverage, whether negative or positive.

OUTLOOK

Although city management is a growing profession, the field is still relatively small. The U.S. Department of Labor predicts that employment at the local government level will increase by approximately 11 percent through 2014, which is at a rate somewhat slower than the average for all occupations. One reason for this is that few new governments are likely to form and, therefore, there will be few new job openings. Applicants with only a bachelor's degree will have the most difficulty finding employment. Even an entry-level job often requires an advanced degree. The ICMA provides funds to those cities wanting to establish the county-manager form of government, as well as to cities where the form is threatened.

City managers are finding that they are sharing more and more of their authority with many different groups, such as unions and special interest groups. "This dilutes the system," Michael Roberto says, "and makes it harder to manage."

The issues that affect a city are constantly changing. Future city managers will need to focus on clean air regulations, promoting diversity, providing affordable housing, creating new policing methods, and revitalizing old downtown areas.

FOR MORE INFORMATION

For statistics and internship opportunities, contact
   International City/County Management Association
   777 North Capitol Street, NE, Suite 500
   Washington, DC 20002-4201
   Tel: 202-289-4262
   http://www.icma.org

For more information on finding a school, the M.P.A. degree, and public affairs work, contact
   National Association of Schools of Public Affairs and Administration
   1120 G Street, NW, Suite 730
   Washington, DC 20005-3801
   Tel: 202-628-8965
   Email: naspaa@naspaa.org
   http://www.naspaa.org

For information on policy and legislative issues, membership, and conferences, contact
   National League of Cities
   1301 Pennsylvania Avenue, NW, Suite 550
   Washington, DC 20004-1701
   Tel: 202-626-3000
   Email: info@nlc.org
   http://www.nlc.org

Congressional Aides

OVERVIEW

Congressional aides are the men and women who staff the offices of the members of the United States Congress. Working for senators and representatives, they assist with a variety of congressional duties, from administrative details to extensive research on legislation. Members of Congress typically include among their staff an administrative assistant, legislative assistants, a press secretary, an office manager, a personal secretary, and a legislative correspondent. Aides are generally divided into two groups: personal staff and committee staff. An aide may work in an office in Washington, D.C., or in a local district or state office.

HISTORY

Ever since members of Congress first began to hire stenographers and receptionists to assist with office duties, the role of congressional aides has stirred controversy. In the early 1800s, Congressmen worried they would look incapable of handling the responsibilities of their own jobs if they relied too much on assistants. This concern still exists today. Some members of Congress complain that having too many aides distances the senators and representatives from constituents, legislation, and the general requirements of their work.

Even these critics, however, admit that aides are very important to the lawmaking process. Since the end of World War II, with improvements in communications and transportation, voters have been making

22

greater demands on their elected officials. Also, issues and casework have become increasingly complex. The Legislative Reorganization Act of 1946 was passed to allow each House and Senate standing committee to employ a campaign staff of four professional and six clerical workers. Another Reorganization Act passed years later, in 1970, which increased the number of professional staff to six members. The number of staff members has continued to grow, causing Congress to allocate more funds to construct new housing and office space.

THE JOB

Congressional aides see the lawmaking process at work—sometimes right on the Senate floor where laws are made. They work at the sides of important lawmakers, briefing them on legislation. The members of Congress (senators and representatives) rely on aides to assist them with a number of their responsibilities. Many constituents (the voters who elected members to Congress) rely on aides to help them make their voices and opinions heard. Aides answer letters, e-mails, and phone calls, and distribute information to keep Congress members and the people they represent updated on the issues of national and local concern.

John Newsome worked on the staff of Congresswoman Barbara Lee as both a press secretary and legislative aide. Congresswoman Lee serves as the representative of California's 9th district and has been behind many important actions since taking office in April of 1998. Lee was involved in declaring an HIV crisis in the local African-American community, making Alameda County the first jurisdiction in the nation to issue such a declaration. She helped get a grant from the U.S. Department of Commerce for BAYTRADE, an organization that promotes the development of trade relations between Northern California and the African continent. She has also played a part in modifying and passing a bill authorizing a study of the barriers that women face in science, math, and technical fields. It is the job of the congressional aide to inform the public and the media of these actions and also to prepare Congresswoman Lee for press conferences and interviews. During his time at the office, Newsome did just that and also researched legislation. "I've been interested in politics all my life," Newsome says. "I wanted to work for someone with a real eye to grassroots advocacy." When Congress was in session, his days started at around 9:30 A.M. and lasted until 9:00 P.M. or even as late as 11:30 P.M.

In the office of a senator or representative, aides either serve on a personal or committee staff. A basic difference between the two types of staff is that the committee staffs are more strictly concerned with work that involves the construction and passage of legislation, while the personal staffs also deal with matters concerning the home state. Personal aides are generally loyal supporters of their members of Congress and their political philosophies. But this doesn't mean that aides don't sometimes have differing views. In some cases, aides may be more familiar with an issue and the general opinions of the constituents concerning an issue than the member of Congress. An aide's opinion can have an impact on a Congress member's decision.

The most important aide to a Congress member is the *chief of staff*, or *administrative assistant*. Those who achieve this position have worked closely with a Congress member for some time and have gained his or her trust and respect. The Congress member relies on the chief of staff's or administrative assistant's opinion and understanding of politics, legislation, and individual bills when making decisions. These aides also oversee the work of the other congressional aides.

The actual running of the office is handled by *office managers*. They attend to the management of office clerical staff, which includes hiring, staff scheduling, and other personnel matters. In addition to *administrative assistant secretaries* who provide clerical support to the chief of staff, a congressional staff also includes *personal secretaries*. They attend to the Congress member's administrative and clerical needs, which include daily scheduling, expense accounts, and personal correspondence. This correspondence is delivered by *mailroom managers* who are responsible for devising plans for handling the enormous crush of mail that arrives in congressional offices each day. They maintain mass mailing records and prepare reports on mail volume and contents.

The legislative staff in a congressional office assists the Congress member with research of bills and other legislative duties. The *legislative director* directs the legislative staff and helps the Congress member keep up to date on important bills. They make sure the Congress member can make informed decisions on issues. Assisting the director are *legislative assistants* and *legislative correspondents*. Legislative assistants are each responsible for the coverage of issues in which they have developed some expertise. They brief the member of Congress on the status of legislation for which they are responsible and prepare floor statements and amendments for them; they may also write speeches for the member. Legislative correspondents are responsible for researching and drafting responses to letters received in the Congress member's offices.

Press secretaries are the primary spokespersons for members of Congress in their dealings with the media and the public. They respond to daily inquiries from the press, plan media coverage, coordinate press conferences, prepare press releases, and review daily newspapers.

State and district directors are responsible for state or district office operations, helping the Congress member to maintain close interaction with constituents. They represent their Congress member in all areas of the state or district and keep the office in Washington, D.C., informed on issues important to the local voters. Directors also plan the Congress member's visits to the state, sometimes accompanying him or her on a state tour.

A congressional staff also includes *schedulers,* who handle all the Congress member's scheduling of appointments; *computer operators,* who are responsible for computerized correspondence systems; and *caseworkers,* who work directly with people having difficulties with the federal government in such areas as veterans' claims, social security, and tax returns.

REQUIREMENTS
High School
A careful understanding of the government and how it works is important to anyone working for a member of Congress. You should take courses in U.S. government, political science, civics, social studies, and history and get involved in school government and school committees. Attend formal meetings of various school clubs to learn about parliamentary procedure. Writing press releases and letters, and researching current issues are important aspects of congressional work. Journalism classes and reporting for your school newspaper will develop these communication skills.

Postsecondary Training
A well-rounded college education is very important for this career. Many congressional aides, such as chiefs of staff and legislative directors, have graduate degrees or law degrees. Consider undergraduate programs in history, political science, journalism, or economics. Political science programs offer courses in government, political theory, international relations, sociology, and public speaking. Look for internship opportunities in local, state, and federal government and in political campaigns. Journalism programs offer courses in news reporting, communications law, and editing. Contact the offices of your state's members of Congress about applying for internships.

Other Requirements
Congressional aides need good problem-solving skills. They must have leadership abilities as well as the ability to follow instructions. Communication skills are very important, including writing, speaking, and listening. Before working as press secretary, John Newsome

held other writing-related jobs, which involved writing grants and writing for the media. "I'm a very detail-oriented writer," he says. "I love writing. But to get a story sold also requires networking and advocacy. You have to maintain good relationships with people."

Aides must have a good temperament to deal with the stress of preparing a congressperson for voting sessions, and patience when dealing with constituents who have serious concerns about political issues. As with any job in politics, diplomacy is important in helping a Congress member effectively serve a large constituency with widely varying views.

EXPLORING

An extremely valuable—but highly competitive—learning opportunity is to work as a *page*. Pages serve members of Congress, running messages across Capitol Hill. The length of a page's service varies from one summer to one year. Students at least 16 years old are eligible to apply. Contact your state's senator or representative for an application.

You can also gain some insight into the work of a congressional aide through local efforts: volunteer for various school committees, take an active part in clubs, and become involved in school government. Campaigns for local elections rely a lot on volunteers, so find out about ways you can support your favorite candidate. Keep a close watch over current events by reading newspapers and news magazines. With an understanding of current issues, you can take a stand and express your opinions to your local, state, and federal representatives. An annual publication called the *Congressional Staff Directory* (http://www.csd.cq.com/scripts/index.cfm) contains the addresses, phone numbers, and biographical information for members of Congress and their aides. You can use this directory to express your views on an issue to your representatives. By contacting your Congress members' offices, you'll be talking to congressional aides and learning something about their responsibilities. (Print or online versions of this directory are available for purchase.)

EMPLOYERS

Congressional aides are federal employees. There are 100 senators and 435 representatives who hire congressional aides. This number won't change without an amendment to the constitution or the addition of another state. For fair representation in the U.S. Congress, each state is allowed two senators; the number of representatives for each state is determined by the state's population. California has the most representatives (53). Most congressional aides work on Capitol Hill in Washington, D.C. Some find work in the home-state offices of their members of Congress.

STARTING OUT

Assistants are needed at every level of government. While in college, make personal contacts by volunteering on political campaigns. But be prepared to volunteer your services for some time in order to advance into positions of responsibility for candidates and elected officials. John Newsome has been involved since high school in grass-roots advocacy. Over the years, he's been involved in HIV activism and community service with mentally disabled youth. Experience with these issues helped him to get his job with Congresswoman Lee. You can also gain valuable experience working in the offices of your state capitol building. State legislators require aides to answer phones, send letters, and research new bills.

Become familiar with the *Congressional Staff Directory,* available at your library or online. Getting a job as a congressional aide can be a difficult task—you may need to regularly submit résumés to placement offices of the House and the Senate. An internship can be a great way to get a foot in the door. The Congressional Manage ment Foundation publishes information on internships.

ADVANCEMENT

Advancement in any of the congressional aide jobs is directly related to a congressional aide's ability, experience on Capitol Hill, and willingness to make personal sacrifices to complete work efficiently and on time. The highest office on congressional staffs is that of administrative assistant. It is possible for anyone on staff to rise up through the ranks to fill this position. Obviously, everyone cannot reach the top position, but advancement to higher staff positions is available to those who show they have the ability to take on greater responsibility. Legislative directors and state and district directors are probably the most likely candidates for the job of chief of staff. Legislative assistants, state office managers, and district office managers are in the best position to move into their respective directors' jobs. The top secretarial position is that of personal secretary, and any of the other secretaries can aspire to that position or that of scheduler. Any of the administrative staff, such as the receptionist or the mail room manager, can work toward the office manager's position.

EARNINGS

Congressional aides' salaries vary a great deal from office to office. Aides working in Senate positions generally have higher salaries than those working in House positions. Earnings also vary by position. A chief of staff, for example, has a much higher salary than a staff assistant working in the same office. Experience also plays a role in aides' earnings, with the highest salaries going to staffers with the most experience. Additionally, aides' earnings vary by the location of the office, that is, Washington, D.C., or the Congress person's home district, in which they work.

The Congressional Management Foundation (CMF), a nonprofit organization in Washington, D.C., publishes periodic reports on congressional employment practices that include salary information. According to the CMF study *Senate Salary, Tenure & Demographic Data,* 1991–2001, the average annual salary for all Senate positions (including congressional aides) was $49,236 in 2001. In 2000 (the most recent data available), the average House salary for all positions was $42,314. These averages are for positions in Washington, D.C. CMF's *2000 House Staff Employment Study* found that the average annual salary for a House chief of staff was $97,615. House office managers averaged $44,009; systems administrators averaged $30,205; and staff assistants averaged $23,849. Again, these averages are for positions in Washington, D.C. More information on these reports is available from the CMF at http://www.cmfweb.org.

WORK ENVIRONMENT

Oddly enough, while Congress makes laws to protect workers and to ensure civil rights among the general populace, it has, in many cases, exempted itself from such laws. Members of Congress contend that they should not be regulated like firms in the private sector because of the political nature of their institution and the necessity of choosing staff on the basis of loyalty. They also feel that it would breach the principle of the separation of powers if the executive branch had the power to enforce labor regulations in Congress.

Congressional aides are often faced with long hours, cramped quarters, and constant pressure. But many people thrive on the fast pace and appreciate the opportunity to get to know federal legislation from the inside. "The opportunities to meet people are endless," John Newsome says. "And it's incredibly challenging work." Despite the high pressure and deadlines, Newsome liked being a member of a staff involved in making positive changes.

OUTLOOK

Members of Congress will continue to hire aides regularly; however, this is not a large employment field. The need for new workers will be steady but limited. Additionally, aides' positions are linked to the success of the congressman or congresswoman for whom they work. If their employer is voted out of office, aides also lose their jobs. And, despite the long hours and often low pay, these jobs are prestigious, making competition for them strong.

Few people make working as a congressional aide a lifelong career. Those with excellent educational backgrounds and who are comfortable using technologies should have the best chances for jobs. The Internet is making it easier for constituents to express their views quickly and to access press releases, information about current legislation, and the positions of their representatives. Advocacy groups will expand their use of the Internet, gaining more support and encouraging voters to express their views via email. In the future, aides will work with a constituency much more knowledgeable about current legislation. The Internet will also serve aides in their research of bills, their interaction with the media, and their gauging of public views.

FOR MORE INFORMATION

For more information about House and Senate employment studies and other publications, such as Congressional Intern Handbook, *contact*

Congressional Management Foundation
513 Capitol Court, NE, Suite 300
Washington, DC 20002-7709
Tel: 202-546-0100
Email: cmf@cmfweb.org
http://www.cmfweb.org

Visit the Web sites of the House and the Senate for extensive information about individual Congress members and legislation. To write to your Congress members, contact

Office of Senator (Name)
U.S. Senate
Washington, DC 20510
http://www.senate.gov

Office of Congressperson (Name)
U.S. House of Representatives
Washington, DC 20510
http://www.house.gov

For employment opportunities, mail your resume and cover letters to
Senate Placement Office
Room SH-142B
Washington, DC 20510

U.S. House of Representatives
Office of Human Resources
B72 Ford House Office Building
Washington, DC 20515-6610

Customs Officials

OVERVIEW

Customs officials are federal workers employed by the United States Bureau of Customs and Border Protection (an arm of the Department of Homeland Security) to prevent terrorists and terrorist weapons from entering the United States, enforce laws governing imports and exports, and combat smuggling and revenue fraud. The Bureau of Customs and Border Protection generates revenue for the government by assessing and collecting duties and excise taxes on imported merchandise. Amid a whirl of international travel and commercial activity, customs officials process travelers, baggage, cargo, and mail, as well as administer certain navigation laws.

Stationed in the United States and overseas at airports, seaports, and all crossings, as well as at points along the Canadian and Mexican borders, customs officials examine, count, weigh, gauge, measure, and sample commercial and noncommercial cargoes entering and leaving the United States. It is their job to determine whether or not goods are admissible and, if so, how much tax, or duty, should be assessed on them. To prevent smuggling, fraud, and cargo theft, customs officials also check the individual baggage declarations of international travelers and oversee the unloading of all types of commercial shipments. More than 40,000 customs workers are employed by the Bureau of Customs and Border Protection.

QUICK FACTS

School Subjects
English
Government

Personal Skills
Communication/ideas
Helping/teaching

Work Environment
Primarily indoors
Primarily one location

Minimum Education Level
High school diploma

Salary Range
$25,195 to $46,189 to $55,360+

Certification or Licensing
None available

Outlook
About as fast as the average

DOT
168

GOE
04.03.01

NOC
1236

O*NET-SOC
33-3021.05

HISTORY

Countries collect taxes on imports and sometimes on exports as a means of producing revenue for the government. Export duties were introduced in England in the year 1275 by a statute that levied taxes on animal hides and on wool. American colonists in the 1700s objected to the import duties England forced them to pay (levied under the Townshend Acts), charging "taxation without representation." Although the British government rescinded the Townshend Acts, it retained the tax on tea, which led to the Boston Tea Party on December 16, 1773.

After the American Revolution, delegates at the Constitutional Convention decided that "no tax or duty shall be laid on articles exported from any state," but they approved taxing imports from abroad. The customs service was established by the First Congress in 1789 as part of the Treasury Department. Until 1816 these customs assessments were used primarily for revenue. The Tariff Act of 1816 declared, however, that the main function of customs laws was to protect American industry from foreign companies. By 1927 the customs service was established as a separate bureau within the Treasury Department.

The terrorist attacks of 2001 prompted a restructuring of many governmental agencies, including the U.S. Customs Service. In 2003, the U.S. Customs Service was renamed the Bureau of Customs and Border Protection (CBP) and merged with portions of the Department of Agriculture, the Immigration and Naturalization Service, and the Border Patrol. CBP became an official agency of the Department of Homeland Security on March 1, 2003.

Today, the Bureau of Customs and Border Protection oversees more than 400 laws and regulations and generates more government money than any other federal agency besides the Internal Revenue Service.

THE JOB

Customs officials perform a wide variety of duties, including preventing terrorists and terrorist weapons from entering the United States, controlling imports and exports, and combating smuggling and revenue fraud.

As a result of its merger in 2003 with several other protective and monitoring agencies of the U.S. government, the Bureau of Customs and Border Patrol has created a new position, the *Customs and Border Patrol (CBP) Officer,* which consolidates the skills and responsibilities of three positions in these agencies: the customs inspector, the immigration officer, and the agricultural inspector. These workers are uniformed and armed. A second new position, the *CBP Agriculture Specialist*, has been created to complement the work of the CBP Officer. CBP Agriculture Specialists are uniformed but not armed.

CBP Officers conduct surveillance at points of entry into the United States to prohibit smuggling, detect customs violations, and deter acts of terrorism. They try to catch people illegally transporting smuggled merchandise and contraband such as narcotics, watches, jewelry, chemicals, and weapons, as well as fruits, plants, and meat that may be infested with pests or diseases. On the waterfront, officers monitor piers, ships, and crew members and are constantly on the lookout for items being thrown from the ship to small boats nearby. Customs patrol officers provide security at entrance and exit facilities of piers and airports, make sure all baggage is checked, and maintain security at loading, exit, and entrance areas of customs buildings and during the transfer of legal drug shipments to prevent hijackings or theft. Using informers and other sources, they gather intelligence information about illegal activities. When probable cause exists, they are authorized to take possible violators into custody, using physical force or weapons if necessary. They assist other customs personnel in developing or testing new enforcement techniques and equipment.

CBP Officers also are responsible for carefully and thoroughly examining cargo to make sure that it matches the description on a ship's or aircraft's manifest. They inspect baggage and personal items worn or carried by travelers entering or leaving the United States by ship, plane, or automobile. CBP Officers are authorized to go aboard a ship or plane to determine the exact nature of the cargo being transported. In the course of a single day, they review cargo manifests, inspect cargo containers, and supervise unloading activities to prevent terrorism, smuggling, fraud, or cargo thefts. They may have to weigh and measure imports to see that commerce laws are being followed and to protect American distributors in cases where restricted trademarked merchandise is brought into the country. In this way, they can protect the interests of American companies.

CBP Officers examine crew and passenger lists, sometimes in cooperation with the police or security personnel from federal government agencies, who may be searching for criminals or terrorists. They are authorized to search suspicious individuals and to arrest these offenders if necessary. They are also allowed to conduct body searches of suspected individuals to check for contraband. They check health clearances and ships' documents in an effort to prevent the spread of disease that may require quarantine.

Individual baggage declarations of international travelers also come under their scrutiny. CBP Officers who have baggage examination duties at points of entry into the United States classify purchases made

Customs and Border Protection Officers examine inbound cargo from a foreign country. *(U.S. Customs and Border Protection)*

abroad and, if necessary, assess and collect duties. All international travelers are allowed to bring home certain quantities of foreign purchases, such as perfume, clothing, tobacco, and liquor, without paying taxes. However, they must declare the amount and value of their purchases on a customs form. If they have made purchases above the duty-free limits, they must pay taxes. CBP Officers are prepared to advise tourists about U.S. customs regulations and allow them to change their customs declarations if necessary and pay the duty before baggage inspection. CBP Officers must be alert and observant to detect undeclared items. If any are discovered, it is up to the officer to decide whether an oversight or deliberate fraud has occurred. Sometimes the contraband is held and a hearing is scheduled to decide the case. A person who is caught trying to avoid paying duty is fined. When customs violations occur, officers must file detailed reports and often later appear as witnesses in court.

CBP Agriculture Specialists inspect agricultural and related goods that are imported into the United States. They act as agricultural experts at ports of entry to help protect people from agroterrorism and bioterrorism, as well as monitor agricultural imports for diseases and harmful pests.

CBP Officers and CBP Agriculture Specialists cooperate with special agents for the Federal Bureau of Investigation (FBI), the Drug

Enforcement Administration, the Food and Drug Administration, and other government agencies.

Some other specialized careers in the Bureau of Customs and Border Protection are as follows:

Customs pilots, who must have a current Federal Aviation Administration (FAA) commercial pilot's license, conduct air surveillance of illegal traffic crossing U.S. borders by air, land, or sea. They apprehend, arrest, and search violators and prepare reports used to prosecute the criminals. They are stationed along the Canadian and Mexican borders as well as along coastal areas, flying single- and multi-engine planes and helicopters.

Canine enforcement officers train and use dogs to prevent smuggling of all controlled substances as defined by customs laws. These controlled substances include marijuana, narcotics, and dangerous drugs. After undergoing an intensive 15-week basic training course in the National Detector Dog Training Center, where each officer is paired with a dog and assigned to a post, canine enforcement officers work in cooperation with CBP Officers to find and seize contraband and arrest smugglers. Canine enforcement officers also use dogs to detect bomb-making materials or other dangerous substances.

Import specialists become technical experts in a particular line of merchandise, such as wine or electronic equipment. They keep up to date on their area of specialization by going to trade shows and importers' places of business. Merchandise for delivery to commercial importers is examined, classified, and appraised by these specialists who must enforce import quotas and trademark laws. They use import quotas and current market values to determine the unit value of the merchandise in order to calculate the amount of money due the government in tariffs. Import specialists routinely question importers, check their lists, and make sure the merchandise matches the description and the list. If they find a violation, they call for a formal inquiry by customs special agents. Import specialists regularly deal with problems of fraud and violations of copyright and trademark laws. If the importer meets federal requirements, the import specialist issues a permit that authorizes the release of merchandise for delivery. If not, the goods might be seized and sold at public auction. These specialists encourage international trade by authorizing the lowest allowable duties on merchandise.

Customs and Border Protection chemists form a subgroup of import specialists who protect the health and safety of Americans. They analyze imported merchandise for textile fibers, lead content, narcotics, and the presence of explosives or other harmful material. In many cases, the duty collected on imported products depends on the chemist's analysis and subsequent report. Customs chemists often serve as expert witnesses in court. Customs laboratories have specialized instruments that can analyze materials for their chemical components. These machines can determine such things as the amount of sucrose in a beverage, the fiber content of a textile product, the lead oxide content of fine crystal, and the presence of toxic chemicals and prohibited additives.

Criminal investigators, or *special agents,* are plainclothes investigators who make sure that the government obtains revenue on imports and that contraband and controlled substances do not enter or leave the country illegally. They investigate smuggling, criminal fraud, and major cargo thefts. Special agents target professional criminals as well as ordinary tourists who give false information on baggage declarations. Often working undercover, they cooperate with CBP Officers and the FBI. Allowed special powers of entry, search, seizure, and arrest, special agents have the broadest powers of search of any law enforcement personnel in the United States. For instance, special agents do not need probable cause or a warrant to justify search or seizure near a border or port of entry. However, in the interior of the United States, probable cause but not a warrant is necessary to conduct a search.

REQUIREMENTS

High School
If you are interested in working for the U.S. Bureau of Customs and Border Protection, you should pursue a well-rounded education in high school. Courses in government, geography and social studies, English, and history will contribute to your understanding of international and domestic legal issues as well as giving you a good general background. If you wish to become a specialist in scientific or investigative aspects of the CBP, courses in the sciences, particularly chemistry, will be necessary, and courses in computer science will be helpful. Taking a foreign language, especially Spanish, will also help prepare you for this career.

Postsecondary Training
Applicants to CBP must be U.S. citizens and at least 21 years of age. They must have earned at least a high school diploma, but applicants with college degrees are preferred. Applicants are required to have three years of general work experience involving contact with the public or four years of college.

Like all federal employees, applicants to CBP must pass a physical examination, undergo a security check, and pass a written test.

Entrance-level appointments are at grades GS-5 and GS-7, depending on the level of education or work experience.

New CBP Officers participate in a rigorous training program that includes 10 days of pre-Academy orientation; 12 weeks of basic training; In-Port Training (a combination of on-the-job, computer-based and classroom training); and Advanced Proficiency Training. CBP Agricultural Specialists receive specialized training from the U.S. Department of Agriculture.

Other Requirements

Applicants must be in good physical condition, possess emotional and mental stability, and demonstrate the ability to correctly apply regulations or instructional material and make clear, concise oral or written reports.

EXPLORING

There are several ways for you to learn about the various positions available at CBP. You can read *CBP Today* (http://www.customs.ustreas.gov/xp/cgov/toolbox/publications), the official employee newsletter of the United States Bureau of Customs and Border Protection, to learn more about customs work. You can also talk with people employed as customs workers, consult your high school counselors, or contact local labor union organizations and offices for additional information. Information on federal government jobs is available from offices of the state employment service, area offices of the U.S. Office of Personnel Management, and Federal Job Information Centers throughout the country.

Another great way to learn more about this career is to participate in the CBP Explorer Program. CBP Explorers receive practical and hands-on training in law enforcement and criminal justice fields. Applicants must be between the ages of 14 and 21 and have at least a C grade point average in high school or college. Participation in this program is also an excellent starting point for entry into the field. After one year in the program, Explorers can apply to the U.S. Customs Explorer Academy.

EMPLOYERS

The U.S. Customs Service is the sole employer of customs officials. More than 40,000 customs officials are employed in the United States.

STARTING OUT

Applicants may enter the various occupations of the Bureau of Customs and Border Protection by applying to take the appropriate civil service examinations. Interested applicants should note the age, citizenship, and experience requirements previously described and realize that they will undergo a background check and a drug test. If hired, applicants will receive exacting on-the-job training.

ADVANCEMENT

All customs agents have the opportunity to advance through a special system of promotion from within. Although they enter at the GS-5 or GS-7 level, after one year they may compete for promotion to supervisory positions or simply to positions at a higher grade level in the agency. The journeyman level is grade GS-9. Supervisory positions at GS-11 and above are available on a competitive basis. After attaining permanent status (i.e., serving for one year on probation), customs patrol officers may compete to become special agents. Entry-level appointments for customs chemists are made at GS-5. However, applicants with advanced degrees or professional experience in the sciences, or both, should qualify for higher graded positions. Advancement potential exists for the journeyman level at GS-11 and to specialist, supervisory, and management positions at grades GS-12 and above.

EARNINGS

Entry-level positions at GS-5 began at a base annual pay of $25,195 in 2006, and entry at GS-7 started at $31,209 per year. Most CBP Officers are at the GS-11 position, which had a base annual salary of $46,189 in 2006. Supervisory positions beginning at GS-12 started at $55,360 in 2006. Federal employees in certain cities receive locality pay in addition to their salaries in order to offset the higher cost of living in those areas. Locality pay generally adds from 8.64 percent to 19.04 percent to the base salary. Certain CBP workers are also entitled to receive Law Enforcement Availability Pay, which adds another 25 percent to their salaries. All federal workers receive annual cost-of-living salary increases. Federal workers enjoy generous benefits, including health and life insurance, pension plans, and holiday, sick leave, and vacation pay.

WORK ENVIRONMENT

The customs territory of the United States is divided into nine regions that include the 50 states, the District of Columbia, Puerto

Rico, and the U.S. Virgin Islands. In these regions there are some 317 ports of entry along land and sea borders. Customs inspectors may be assigned to any of these ports or to overseas work at airports, seaports, waterfronts, border stations, customs houses, or the U.S. Bureau of Customs and Border Protection Headquarters in Washington, D.C. They are able to request assignments in certain localities and usually receive them when possible.

A typical work schedule is eight hours a day, five days a week, but CBP Officers and related employees often work overtime or long into the night. United States entry and exit points must be supervised 24 hours a day, which means that workers rotate night shifts and weekend duty. CBP Officers are sometimes assigned to one-person border points at remote locations, where they may perform immigration and agricultural inspections in addition to regular duties. They often risk physical injury from criminals violating customs regulations.

OUTLOOK

Employment at the Bureau of Customs and Border Protection is steady work that is not affected by changes in the economy. With the increased emphasis on law enforcement, especially the deterrence of terrorism but also the detection of illegally imported drugs and pornography and the prevention of exports of sensitive high-technology items, the prospects for steady employment in the CBP are likely to grow and remain high. The U.S. Department of Labor predicts employment for police and detectives, a category including CBP Officers, to grow as fast as the average through 2014.

FOR MORE INFORMATION

For career information and to view a short video about CBP Officers, visit the CBP Web site:
   U.S. Customs and Border Protection (CBP)
   Department of Homeland Security
   1300 Pennsylvania Avenue, NW
   Washington, DC 20229-0001
   Tel: 202-354-1000
   http://www.customs.ustreas.gov

Deputy
U.S. Marshals

QUICK FACTS

School Subjects
Computer science
Foreign language
Government

Personal Skills
Helping/teaching
Leadership/management

Work Environment
Indoors and outdoors
Primarily multiple locations

Minimum Education Level
High school diploma

Salary Range
$25,195 to $31,209 to
$118,957

Certification or Licensing
None available

Outlook
Faster than the average

DOT
377

GOE
04.03.01

NOC
N/A

O*NET-SOC
N/A

OVERVIEW

The United States Marshals Service forms a central part of the federal government's law enforcement efforts. As a bureau within the Department of Justice, the Marshals Service reports to the U.S. attorney general. Among the responsibilities of *deputy U.S. marshals* are providing court security, which includes personal protection of judges, judicial officials, and jurors; serving warrants and process documents; locating and apprehending fugitives; transporting prisoners; managing the federal Witness Security Program; seizing assets used in or resulting from criminal activity; and handling special assignments and operations. There are approximately 3,065 deputy U.S. marshals employed throughout the United States.

HISTORY

The U.S. Marshals Service has its roots in the Judiciary Act, passed by Congress in 1789, which established not only the post of U.S. marshal but also the country's original federal court system. The act delegated two duties to the marshals: to enforce all precepts issued by the federal government and to protect and attend to the federal courts. Marshals were also authorized to hire one or more deputies.

The first 13 U.S. marshals, appointed by President George Washington, were confirmed by the U.S. Senate on September 26, 1789. Over the next year, two more marshals were chosen. The 13 original states, as well as the districts of Kentucky and Maine, were each assigned a marshal to represent the federal government's interests at a local level. The number of marshals and deputies increased as the United States expanded westward, and with a rise in the country's population, some states were assigned more than one marshal. By the 2000s, there were approximately 3,065 deputy U.S. marshals assigned to the 94 federal judicial districts across the United States and Puerto Rico, Guam, the Virgin Islands, and the Northern Marianas.

The duties of the Marshals Service expanded soon after the appointment of the first marshals. Marshals and deputies were required, for example, to play a major role in taking the national census (a responsibility that lasted until 1870), to supervise federal penitentiaries in the western territories, to enforce precepts from the French consuls, to take custody of goods seized by customs officers, and to sell seized lands. Along with the increase in responsibilities came a corresponding growth in the number of superiors to whom the Marshals Service was accountable. By the mid-19th century, the federal courts, the secretary of the treasury, the solicitor of the treasury, and the secretary of the interior all had supervisory powers over some aspects of the work of the marshals and deputies. In 1861, however, the Marshals Service came under the exclusive power of the attorney general, and in 1870 the service became a part of the newly created Department of Justice.

U.S. marshals and their deputies have frequently faced potentially dangerous situations. The level of danger was especially great in the 19th century for those who were charged with keeping order in newly established western territories. During the Oklahoma land rush, for example, more than 60 marshals were killed in a span of just five years. It is the Marshals Service of the late 19th century—the time of legendary marshals Bat Masterson and Wyatt Earp—dramatized in numerous books and films about the role of marshals and deputies in the Old West. Some might also remember that marshals and deputies were charged with quelling civil disturbances such as the Whisky Rebellion of 1791, the Pullman Strike of 1894, and the antiwar protests of the late 1960s; enforcing school integration beginning in the 1960s; and confronting militant Native Americans at Wounded Knee, South Dakota, in 1973. Today, the men and women of the Marshals Service, trained in the latest techniques and equipment, continue to perform a wide variety of law enforcement and homeland security duties under the attorney general and the U.S. Department of Justice.

THE JOB

One of the oldest duties of the U.S. Marshals Service is court security. Originally, this entailed the presence of a marshal or deputy in the courtroom to maintain order and to ensure the safety of the judge. In time, however, the job of protecting the courts has become much more complex. Now, depending on the trial, prosecutors, attorneys, jurors, witnesses, family members, and any other trial participant potentially in danger might be provided with security. Marshals have been assisted in carrying out these responsibilities by using advanced equipment—high-tech alarm systems, for example—as well as by improved law enforcement techniques. The Marshals Service is sometimes alerted to dangers by threats mentioned in letters or phone calls or by informants, but deputies cannot rely on these explicit means of warning. Constant vigilance is required.

A special area related to court security is the federal Witness Security Program. Witnesses who risk their lives to testify against organized crime figures or others involved in major criminal activity are given around-the-clock protection. After the trial, the witnesses are relocated to another part of the country and given a new identity. The Marshals Service provides support programs to help these witnesses adjust to their new identities and environments.

A significant part of the workload involves serving process documents and executing court orders. Private process-serving companies work for the courts to serve papers for civil cases, but the Marshals Service handles almost all of the criminal process-serving needs of the court. There are many kinds of process documents, including subpoenas, restraining orders, notices of condemnations, and summonses. In the days of the Old West, serving process documents was one of their most dangerous duties, sometimes entailing traveling on horseback for long distances, as well as face-to-face shootouts. Sophisticated equipment, allowing for better means of surveillance and coordination, has made this task less threatening. About 1 million process documents are now handled each year by the Marshals Service.

Even more dangerous are the execution of arrest warrants and the apprehension of fugitives. Along with other federal agencies, such as the Federal Bureau of Investigation (FBI), the Marshals Service continues to perform these tasks, handling more than 44,000 arrest warrants each year and apprehending more fugitives than all other federal law enforcement agencies combined. The Marshals Service is responsible for locating and apprehending many types of fugitives, including parole and probation violators and prisoners who have escaped from federal prisons.

For most of its history, the Marshals Service has been charged with the responsibility of seizing, managing, and disposing of property involved in criminal cases. Many of these cases now involve drug trafficking. Planes, cars, boats, houses and condominiums, ranches, businesses, and restaurants, as well as personal assets such as jewelry and cash, are some examples of the type of property seized. Property seized in this manner is forfeited under the law and then sold off at public auctions or by other means. Seized property may also be transferred to law enforcement agencies for official use.

The Marshals Service is also in charge of transporting federal prisoners. Using automobiles, buses, vans, and aircraft—some of them obtained by the asset seizure program—U.S. Marshals supervise the movements of more than 300,000 prisoners each year. After a trial, convicts awaiting a sentence are also the responsibility of the Marshals Service. The average number of prisoners held in custody each day by the Marshals Service is approximately 54,000.

Protecting the shipment of weapons systems is a more recent responsibility. Under an agreement with the United States Air Force, deputies direct traffic and help escort vehicles transporting weapons systems, deterring or arresting anyone who attempts to disrupt the shipment.

Within the Marshals Service is a rapid-deployment force called the Special Operations Group (SOG). The unit was formed in 1971 in order to handle national emergencies, such as civil disturbances, hostage cases, or terrorist attacks. Members of SOG are regular deputies, located in all parts of the country, who are given specialized training and who must always be on call for emergencies.

Fast Facts

In 2005, the U.S. Marshal Service:

- Arrested more than 35,500 federal fugitives and more than 44,000 state/local fugitives.
- Provided security at more than 400 court facilities.
- Facilitated more than 305,000 federal prisoner movements.
- Protected 17,700 witnesses and their families via its Witness Security Program.
- Supervised 168,781 prisoners.
- Had a total of 4,535 employees—94 U.S. marshals, 3,067 deputy marshals, and 1,374 administrative employees and detention enforcement officers.

Source: U.S. Marshals Service

REQUIREMENTS

High School

If you are interested in becoming a deputy U.S. marshal, you must complete high school and obtain an undergraduate degree or equivalent experience. In high school, you should pursue a general course of study that includes courses in government, one or more foreign languages, English, history, and computer science.

Postsecondary Training

The Marshals Service requires that candidates have a minimum level of education or experience. A four-year bachelor's degree in any major is sufficient. Without an undergraduate degree, however, an applicant needs at least three years' experience in a job demonstrating poise and self-confidence under stress, as well as the ability to reason soundly, make decisions quickly, find practical solutions, accept responsibility, interact tactfully with a wide range of people, and prepare reports. Although any number of occupations may fulfill these requirements, the following are examples of acceptable experience: (1) law enforcement; (2) correctional treatment and supervision of inmates; (3) classroom teaching; (4) volunteer work or counseling for a community action program; (5) sales work (but not over-the-counter sales positions); (6) interviewing; or (7) jobs such as a credit rating investigator, claims adjuster, or journalist that require public contact for the purpose of collecting information. For candidates who have been to college but do not have a degree, every year of study is accepted as nine months of experience.

All candidates are required to take a written test of 125 questions. A score of 78 or better is passing. The questions are intended to evaluate clerical skills, the ability to reason verbally, and the level of proficiency in abstract reasoning (that is, using symbols and numbers). Candidates are also given a personal interview and, as for all government jobs, must be willing to undergo an extensive background check.

Once hired, new deputy marshals are sent to a 10-week basic training program at the U.S. Marshals Service Training Academy in Glynco, Georgia. The program features courses in law enforcement, criminal investigation, forensics, and areas particular to the Marshals Service. There are also a rigorous physical fitness program and 18 months of on-the-job training.

Other Requirements

Before being hired, candidates must pass a background investigation, drug test, and medical examination. They must also be U.S. citizens who are between the ages of 21 and 36. Like those in other law enforcement positions, deputy U.S. marshals must be in excellent physical shape, and must pass a Fitness-In-Total assessment. Moreover, their vision must be no worse than 20/200 uncorrected in both eyes (corrected to at least 20/20); they must have good hearing (equivalent to being able to hear a whispered voice at 15 feet); and they may not have insulin-dependent diabetes or any other health condition that might interfere with job performance or endanger the health and safety of others.

EXPLORING

For any law enforcement job, it is difficult to obtain practical experience prior to entering the field. If you are interested in more information about working as a deputy U.S. marshal, you should write directly to the Marshals Service. Many police departments, however, hire student trainees and interns, and this may provide good exposure to general law enforcement. In addition, the FBI operates an Honors Internship Program (https://www.fbijobs.gov/honors. asp) for undergraduate and graduate students selected by the FBI. A school guidance counselor, a college or university career services office, or a public library may also have additional information.

EMPLOYERS

The U.S. Marshals Service is the sole employer of the approximately 3,065 deputy U.S. marshals.

STARTING OUT

The Marshals Service accepts only candidates who have fulfilled the necessary physical, educational, and experiential requirements listed above. Those interested in pursuing the field should contact the Marshals Service to find out when and where the written examination will take place.

Candidates with postsecondary education, particularly undergraduate and graduate degrees in fields related to law, law enforcement, criminology, or political science, will have the strongest chance of joining the U.S. Marshals Service. Knowledge of foreign languages and specialized skills, including computer and electronics skills, are also in high demand by the U.S. Marshals office.

ADVANCEMENT

Advancement is made on the basis of merit and experience. Within a district office, the top position is that of U.S. marshal. Appointed by the president of the United States, U.S. marshals must be confirmed by the U.S. Senate. Directly under the U.S. Marshal is the *Chief Deputy U.S. Marshal,* who oversees the district's staff of supervisors, the deputy U.S. marshals, and the support staff. Each district also employs specialists in witness security, court security, and seized property.

EARNINGS

As with other federal positions, salaries for deputy U.S. marshals are fixed at government service rating levels. Beginning deputy U.S. marshals are generally hired at the GS-5 level, at which an annual salary was between $25,195 and $32,755 in 2006. Deputy U.S. marshals with bachelor's and especially advanced degrees in law enforcement, criminology, law, and other related disciplines may be hired at the GS-7 level, which draws a salary between $31,209 and $40,569. Those appointed at the GS-5 grade level are eligible for promotion to GS-7 after one year, and those appointed at the GS-7 grade level are eligible for promotion to GS-9 after one year.

Top salaries for deputy U.S. marshals are at the GS-11 level, which paid a base rate of $46,189 per year in 2006, but deputy U.S. marshals certified in a specialty area may earn the GS-12 level, which was $55,360 in 2006. The top rating, GS-15, paid $91,507 to $118,957 per year in 2006.

In addition, deputies assigned to certain cities—including New York; Los Angeles; Boston; Miami; San Francisco; Washington, D.C.; Alexandria, Virginia; and others—receive higher pay based on the higher cost of living in these areas. All federal workers receive annual cost-of-living salary increases.

Benefits include health and life insurance, paid vacations and holidays, and a pension program. Most federal law enforcement officials are eligible for early retirement.

WORK ENVIRONMENT

In general, deputy U.S. marshals work 40 hours a week. These hours are usually during the daytime, Monday through Friday, but overtime and other shifts are sometimes required. Travel may be necessary, for example, to transport a prisoner from one state to another.

Deputies generally work out of well-maintained, clean offices, but their duties can take them to a wide variety of environments, such as a courtroom; an automobile, helicopter, or airplane; the streets of a major U.S. city; or, when trying to locate a fugitive, a foreign country.

Like all law enforcement jobs, personal safety is a concern. Those interested in working for the U.S. Marshals Service should be well aware of the potential for physical harm or even death. Because of the danger, deputies carry firearms and are well-trained in self-defense and other paramilitary techniques. Strenuous physical exertion, emotional stress, and exposure to harsh conditions (such as poor weather) are often a part of the job.

For some deputies, an advantage of the job is the diversity of cases. Others find personal satisfaction in knowing that they are serving their country. Deputy U.S. marshals enjoy great respect and confidence from the public.

OUTLOOK

There are close to 3,065 deputy U.S. marshals assigned to the 94 districts across the United States and Puerto Rico, Guam, the Virgin Islands, and the Northern Marianas. Changes in the service's budget, as well as increases or decreases in the responsibilities assigned the service, affect employment opportunities. Careers in law enforcement and security-related fields in general are expected to grow rapidly in some cases, as federal and state governments pass new "tough-on-crime" legislation and the number of criminals continues to grow. Great increases in the crime rate will most likely prompt public pressures to increase hiring of law enforcement officials, including deputy U.S. marshals. Threats of terrorist activity have put all public safety officials on alert, from FBI and CIA experts to local police forces and private security companies. There is now increased security particularly in and around government offices, public buildings, airports, post offices, and media headquarters.

In spite of the continuing need for deputy U.S. marshals, competition for available positions will remain high because of the prestige offered by this career and the generous benefits available to many careers in federal service.

FOR MORE INFORMATION

For information on career opportunities, contact
U.S. Marshals Service
Human Resources Division—Law Enforcement Recruiting
Washington, DC 20530-1000
Tel: 202-307-9600
Email: us.marshals@usdoj.gov
http://www.usdoj.gov/marshals

FBI Agents

QUICK FACTS

School Subjects
English
Foreign language
Government

Personal Skills
Communication/ideas
Leadership/management

Work Environment
Indoors and outdoors
Primarily multiple locations

Minimum Education Level
Bachelor's degree

Salary Range
$42,040 to $65,832 to
$100,000+

Certification or Licensing
None available

Outlook
About as fast as the average

DOT
375

GOE
04.03.01

NOC
N/A

O*NET-SOC
N/A

OVERVIEW

FBI agents, special agents of the Federal Bureau of Investigation (FBI), are employees of the federal government. The FBI is responsible for investigating and enforcing more than 200 federal statutes that encompass terrorism; organized crime; white-collar crime; public corruption; financial crime; government fraud; bribery; copyright matters; civil rights violations; bank robbery; extortion; kidnapping; air piracy; terrorism; foreign counterintelligence; interstate criminal activity; and fugitive and drug-trafficking matters. Agents also conduct background investigations on certain federal government job applicants. There are approximately 11,660 FBI agents employed in the United States.

HISTORY

The Federal Bureau of Investigation was founded in 1908 as the investigative branch of the U.S. Department of Justice. In its earliest years, the FBI's responsibilities were limited. However, the creation of new federal laws gave the FBI jurisdiction over criminal matters that had previously been regulated by the individual states, such as those involving the interstate transportation of stolen vehicles. By the 1920s, the FBI was also used for political purposes such as tracking down alleged subversive elements and spying on political enemies.

Early in its history, the FBI developed a reputation for corruption. In 1924, J. Edgar Hoover was appointed director of FBI and charged with the twin goals of cleaning up the agency and making the agency's work independent from politics. Hoover established

48

stricter professional standards, thus reducing corruption. In addition, partly because of Hoover's own ambitions, the FBI's responsibilities increased. Soon the FBI was the most powerful law enforcement agency in the country.

The FBI established its Identification Division in 1924 and the Bureau's scientific laboratory in 1932. In 1934, the FBI was given the general authority to handle federal crime investigation. Within three years, more than 11,000 federal criminals were convicted through the FBI's efforts. As its prestige grew, the FBI was further designated, in 1939, as the central clearinghouse for all matters pertaining to the internal security of the United States. During World War II, FBI agents rendered many security services for plants involved in war production and worked to gather evidence on espionage activities within the plants.

Since its inception in 1932, the FBI Laboratory has become one of the largest and most comprehensive crime laboratories in the world, providing leadership and service in the scientific solution and prosecution of crimes. It is the only full-service federal forensic laboratory in the United States. As a result, the FBI is involved in a wide variety of law enforcement activities using the latest scientific methods and forms of analysis available.

The FBI's Identification Division serves as the nation's repository and clearinghouse for fingerprint records. The fingerprint section of the FBI Laboratory is the largest in the world, containing millions of sets of fingerprints. In this capacity, the division provides the following services: identifying and maintaining fingerprint records for arrested criminal suspects and for applicants to sensitive jobs; posting notices for people wanted for crimes and for parole or probation violations; examining physical evidence for fingerprints and providing occasional court testimony on the results of examinations; training in fingerprint science; maintaining fingerprint records of people currently reported missing; and identifying amnesia victims and unknown deceased people.

After World War II, the FBI began conducting background security investigations for government agencies, as well as probes into internal security matters for the executive branch of the federal government. The 1960s brought civil rights and organized crime to the forefront for the FBI, and the '70s and '80s focused on counterterrorism, financial crime, drugs, and violent crimes. During the 1990s the FBI continued to focus on these crimes, as well as address the growing threat of cybercrime. The FBI created the Computer Investigations and Infrastructure Threat Assessment Center and other initiatives to respond to physical and cyber attacks against infrastructure in the United States. The FBI's mission changed as a result of the terrorist attacks of September 11, 2001. While still investigating all types of federal crime, the FBI's most important mandate today is to protect the American people from future terrorist attacks.

THE JOB

Formed in 1908, the FBI has the broadest investigative authority of all federal law enforcement agencies. The agency leads long-term, complex investigations while working closely with other federal, state, local, and foreign law enforcement and intelligence agencies.

An FBI special agent is faced with the challenge of investigating and upholding certain federal laws that come under the FBI's jurisdictions. Throughout their career, FBI agents conduct investigations on a variety of issues lumped into the following categories: counterterrorism; counterintelligence; cyber investigations; public corruption; civil rights; organized crime; white-collar crime (such as antitrust investigations, bankruptcy fraud, environmental crime, financial institution fraud, government fraud, health care fraud, insurance fraud, money laundering, securities/commodities fraud, and telemarketing fraud); and major thefts/violent crimes (such as art theft, crimes against children, jewelry and gem theft, and Indian Country crime). FBI agents may be assigned to a wide range of investigations, unless they have specialized skills in a certain area. In short, agents are assigned to a case, conduct an investigation, and then submit a report of their findings to the U.S. Attorney's Office.

During an investigation, agents may use a vast network of communication systems and the bureau's crime detection laboratory to help them with their work. Agents may gather information with the help of the National Crime Information Center and the Criminal Justice Information Services Division. Once they have information, agents must make sure the facts and evidence are correct. FBI agents may discuss their findings with a U.S. attorney or an assistant U.S. attorney, who decides whether the evidence requires legal action. The Justice Department may choose to investigate the matter further, and FBI agents may obtain a search warrant or court order to locate and seize property that may be evidence. If the Justice Department decides to prosecute the case, agents may then obtain an arrest warrant.

With the goal of gathering information and reporting it, FBI agents may spend a considerable amount of time traveling or living in various cities. Their investigations often require them to interview people—witnesses, subjects, or suspects—and search for different types of records. Agents may set up a stakeout to watch a place or person. Special agents may also work with paid informants. Sometimes agents testify in court about their investigations or findings. If enough incriminating evidence is found, FBI agents conduct arrests or raids of various types. Agents must carry firearms while on duty, and they typically carry their bureau identification badge. Agents always carry their credentials. Most of the time, they wear everyday business suits or other appropriate attire—not uniforms.

Some agents with specialized skills may work specific types of investigations, such as fraud or embezzlement. *Language specialists*—who can be employed as special agents or support personnel—may translate foreign language over a wiretap and tape recordings into English. The FBI also employs agents specializing in areas such as chemistry, physics, metallurgy, or computers. *Laboratory specialists* analyze physical evidence such as blood, hair, and body fluids, while others analyze handwriting, documents, and firearms. Agents working for the FBI's Behavioral Science Unit track and profile serial murderers, rapists, and other criminals committing patterned violent crimes.

Agents often work alone, unless the investigation is particularly dangerous or requires more agents. However, FBI agents do not investigate local matters only federal violations that fall within their jurisdiction. Agents' work can be discussed only with other bureau employees, which means they cannot discuss investigations with their families or friends.

The FBI operates 56 field offices, 400 resident agencies, four specialized field installations, and 46 foreign liaison posts. FBI agents must be willing to be reassigned at any point in their career.

REQUIREMENTS

High School

A high school diploma or its equivalent is required. The FBI does not recommend specific courses for high school students. Rather, the bureau encourages students to do the best work they can. Since FBI agents perform a variety of work, numerous academic disciplines are needed.

Postsecondary Training

All special-agent candidates must hold a four-year degree from a college or university accredited by one of the regional or national institutional associations recognized by the U.S. Department of

Education. Candidates must fulfill additional requirements of one of four entry programs: Law, Accounting, Language, and Diversified. Entry through the law program requires a law degree from an accredited resident law school. The accounting program requires a bachelor's degree in accounting or a related discipline such as economics, business, or finance. Applicants for the accounting program must have passed the Uniform Certified Accountant Examination or at least show eligibility to take this exam. Language program applicants may hold a bachelor's degree in any discipline but must demonstrate fluency in one or more foreign languages meeting the current needs of the FBI. In recent years, these languages have included Spanish, Arabic, Farsi, Pashtu, Urdu, Chinese, Japanese, Korean, Vietnamese, and Russian. The diversified program accepts applicants with a bachelor's degree in any discipline plus three years of full-time work experience or an advanced degree accompanied by two years of full-time work experience.

Applicants with law or accounting degrees are especially valued by the FBI. Since agents investigate violations of federal law, a law degree may give applicants an appreciation and understanding of the Federal Rules of Criminal Procedure. Plus, a law degree should help agents identify the elements of a criminal violation and collect the necessary evidence for successful prosecution. Since FBI agents trace financial transactions and review and analyze complex accounting records, an accounting degree will likely help agents document evidence and reveal sophisticated financial crimes.

All candidates must complete a rigorous application process. For those who successfully complete the written tests and interview, the FBI conducts a thorough background investigation that includes credit and criminal record checks; interviews with associates; contact with personal and business references; interviews with past employers and neighbors; and verification of educational achievements. Drug testing and a physical examination are required. A polygraph examination is also required. The completed background investigation is then considered when the final hiring decision is made.

If appointed to the position of an FBI special agent, new hires train for 18 weeks at the FBI Academy in Quantico, Virginia. Agent trainees spend a total of 708 instructional hours studying academic and investigative subjects, and trainees also focus on physical fitness, defensive tactics, and firearms training. Emphasis is placed on developing investigative techniques, as well as skills in interviewing, interrogation, and gathering intelligence information. Agent trainees are tested on their defensive tactics, firearms and weapon handling, physical fitness, and arrest techniques. They must also pass academic exams and obey certain rules and regulations during the training. If the trainees pass the tests at the academy and receive their credentials, they become special agents and are assigned to serve a two-year probationary period at an FBI field office.

After graduation from the FBI Academy, new agents are assigned to an FBI field office for a probationary period lasting one year, after which they become permanent special agents. During the first months of employment, the novice agent is guided by a veteran special agent who will help show how the lessons learned at the academy can be applied on the job. Assignments are determined by the individual's special skills and the current needs of the FBI. As a part of their duties, special agents may be required to relocate during their careers.

The education and training of FBI agents continue throughout their career. FBI agents are always expected to learn new techniques and better methods in criminal investigation, either through experience on the job, advanced study courses, in-service training, or special conferences.

Other Requirements

To qualify for training as an FBI agent, candidates must be U.S. citizens between the ages of 23 and 36. They must possess a valid driver's license, be available for assignment anywhere in the areas of the bureau's jurisdiction (which includes Puerto Rico), and be in excellent physical condition. Their vision must not be worse than 20/200 uncorrected and correctable to 20/20 in one eye and no worse than 20/40 in the other eye. Applicants must also pass a color-vision test and hearing test. Applicants may not have physical disabilities that would interfere with the performance of their duties, including use of firearms and defensive tactics and taking part in raids. All applicants must be able to withstand rigorous physical strain and exertion.

FBI agents assume grave responsibilities as a normal part of their jobs. Their reputation, integrity, and character must be above reproach, and they must be dependable and courageous. Agents must be able to accept continual challenges in their jobs, realizing that no two days of work assignments may be exactly alike. FBI agents need to be stable and personally secure and able to work daily with challenge, change, and danger. For most agents, the FBI is a lifelong career.

EXPLORING

The best method of exploring a career with the FBI is to participate in the FBI Honors Internship Program, held every summer in Washington, D.C. Participation is open to undergraduate and graduate students selected by the FBI. This program is designed to give interns experience and insight into the inner workings of (and career opportunities available at) the FBI. Students are assigned to various divisions of the agency according to their academic disciplines, and they work alongside special agents under the supervision of assistant directors. Interns may work at FBI headquarters or other agency locations in the Washington, D.C., area. Acceptance into the internship program is highly competitive. Applicants must be full-time students intending to return to school after the internship program. They must achieve a cumulative grade point average of 3.0 or higher. Undergraduate applicants must be in their junior year at the time of application. In addition, applicants must submit letters of recommendation and complete a 500-word essay. Undergraduate interns are paid at the GS-6 level, which was approximately $28,085 per year in 2006. Graduate interns are paid at the GS-7 level of about $31,209 in 2006. Transportation to and from Washington, D.C., is also provided as part of the internship program. For more information on this program, visit https://www.fbijobs.gov/honors.asp.

Books to Read

Ackerman, Thomas H. *FBI Careers: The Ultimate Guide to Landing a Job as One of America's Finest.* 2nd ed. Indianapolis, Ind.: JIST Works, 2005.

Baker, Thomas E. *Introductory Criminal Analysis: Crime Prevention and Intervention Strategies.* Upper Saddle River, N.J.: Prentice Hall, 2004.

Bishop, Matt. *Introduction to Computer Security.* Upper Saddle River, N.J.: Addison-Wesley Professional, 2004.

Combs, Cindy C. *Terrorism in the 21st Century.* 3rd ed. Prentice Hall, 2002.

Douglas, John. *John Douglas's Guide to Landing a Career in Law Enforcement.* New York: McGraw-Hill, 2004.

Harr, J. Scott, and Karen M. Hess. *Careers In Criminal Justice And Related Fields: From Internship to Promotion.* 5th ed. Belmont, Calif.: Thomson/Wadsworth, 2005.

Jeffreys, Diarmuid. *The Bureau: Inside the Modern FBI.* Charlotte, N.C.: Replica Books, 2001.

Kessler, Ronald. *The Bureau: The Secret History of the FBI.* New York: St. Martin's Paperbacks, 2003.

In addition to the Honors Internship Program, the FBI offers several other internship opportunities. Visit https://www.fbijobs.gov/intern.asp for more information.

If you are interested in a career with the FBI, you may apply for internships and other programs offered through your local police departments, which will give you experience and insight into aspects of law enforcement in general. Good grades throughout high school and college will give you the best chance of winning a place in the Honors Internship Program.

EMPLOYERS

Agents work for the Federal Bureau of Investigation, which is head-quartered in Washington, D.C., and is the investigative arm of the U.S. Department of Justice. Agents are placed in one of 56 field offices or one of 40 foreign liaison posts. The FBI employed 11,633 special agents as of June 30, 2003. The FBI hires on a continual basis, although some years it does not hire any new agents. When the bureau is hiring, it advertises in newspapers, postings, and the Internet.

STARTING OUT

If you are interested in working for the FBI, contact the applicant coordinator at the FBI field office nearest you, or visit the FBI's job Web site: https://www.fbijobs.gov.

The bureau will send you information on existing vacancies, requirements for the positions, how to file applications, and locations where examinations will be given. Examinations are scored by computer at FBI headquarters. Interviews are arranged based on the applicant's score and overall qualifications, as well as the agency's current needs.

ADVANCEMENT

FBI promotions are awarded mainly on performance rather than seniority. All administrative and supervisory jobs are filled from within the ranks by agents who have demonstrated they are able to handle more responsibility. Some FBI agents climb the ladder to become higher-grade administrators and supervisors. For example, an agent may become an inspector, supervisory special agent, or special agent in charge of a field office. Agents may also be assigned to the FBI headquarters, or they may become headquarters supervisors, unit and section chiefs, and division heads. Agents may retire after 20 years of service and after the age of 50; mandatory retirement is enforced at the age of 57. In some instances, agents may be granted one-year extensions up to the age of 60.

EARNINGS

New FBI agents start out at the federal government's GS-10 level—approximately $42,040 in 2006, depending on where agents live. Salaries for agents are increased slightly if they reside in cities such as New York, Los Angeles, and Miami, which have high costs of living. Agents also receive an additional 25 percent of their base pay (known as law enforcement availability pay or LEAP) as compensation for being available 24 hours a day, seven days a week. FBI agents can earn within-grade pay increases upon satisfactory job performance, and grade increases may be earned as agents gain experience through good job performance. FBI agents in nonsupervisory positions can reach the GS-13 grade—about $65,832 in 2006. Agents who move into management positions can earn a GS-15 salary—about $91,507. Some agents then move into a different employment category called the Senior Executive Service, where they make more than $100,000 annually working for the FBI. Benefits include paid vacation, health and life insurance, retirement, sick leave, and job-related tuition reimbursement.

As federal employees, FBI special agents enjoy generous benefits, including health and life insurance and 13 days of paid sick leave. Vacation pay begins at 13 days for each of the first three years of service and rises to 20 to 26 days for each year after that. All special agents are required to retire at the age of 57; they may choose to retire at 50 if they have put in 20 years of service.

WORK ENVIRONMENT

Depending on their case assignments, FBI agents may work a very strenuous and variable schedule, frequently working more hours than the customary 40-hour week. They are on call for possible assignment 24 hours a day. Assignments may be given for any location at any time. Every aspect of the agent's work is confidential. As a result, agents may work under potentially dangerous circumstances in carrying out their assignments, and they may be confronted with unpleasant and even horrifying aspects of life. Because of the confidential nature of their work, they must refrain from speaking about their casework even with relatives or spouses. In addition, agents may be required to travel and perform their duties under many conditions, including severe weather. Nevertheless, a career with the FBI offers a great deal of respect, responsibility, and the possibility of adventure. No two days are ever the same for a special agent.

OUTLOOK

Most job vacancies within the FBI are expected to come as agents retire, advance, or resign. Turnover, in general, has traditionally been low, as most agents remain with the FBI throughout their working lives.

The numbers of FBI special agents are linked to the scope of the FBI's responsibilities. Increases in organized crimes, white-collar crimes, and terrorist threats on American soil have led the FBI to increase their number of agents in recent years.

As the bureau's responsibilities expand, it will create new positions to meet them. Despite increased recruitment, growth in the numbers of new agency hires is expected to remain somewhat limited. Competition for openings will continue to be extremely high. According to the *Chicago Tribune,* the typical recruit is between the ages of 27 and 31, has a graduate-level education, and is physically fit. Since the terrorist attacks of 2001, the FBI has been particularly interested in recruits who are able to speak Arabic and are familiar with Middle and Far Eastern culture. Potential agents with backgrounds in information technology are also in high demand.

FOR MORE INFORMATION

For information on FBI jobs, internship programs (paid and unpaid), current news, and contact information for a field office in your area, visit the FBI Web site. Contact information for your local field office is also available in your telephone directory.
Federal Bureau of Investigation (FBI)
J. Edgar Hoover Building
935 Pennsylvania Avenue, NW
Washington, DC 20535-0001
Tel: 202-324-3000
http://www.fbi.gov

INTERVIEW

Ross Rice has been an FBI agent for 25 years and is currently assigned to the FBI's Chicago field office. He discussed his career with the editors of Careers in Focus: Government.

Q. Why did you decide to become an FBI agent?

A. I decided to become an FBI agent while I was in high school. I had been following reports of the FBI's investigation into the kidnapping of Patty Hearst and it seemed like an interesting career. The rest, as they say, is history.

Q. Can you describe a typical day on the job?

A. There is really no such thing as a typical day for an FBI agent. What you do is determined by two things: the office to which you are assigned and the type of cases that you're working. There are regular night and weekend assignments no matter what or where you're working.

Q. Do you travel for your job?

A. There is limited travel in the FBI. That's because we have 56 field offices and more than 400 smaller satellite offices located throughout the country and in 46 U.S. embassies worldwide. Most travel is to attend training seminars or for temporary assignments in other offices.

Q. What are some responsibilities that you have as an FBI agent of which the average citizen may not be aware?

A. The FBI is charged by Congress with the investigation of more than 200 violations of federal criminal law. This ranges from the more traditional cases, such as bank robbery and kidnappings, to more recent violations such as terrorism and computer crimes.

Q. How does one train for this career?

A. The basic educational requirement for the special agent position is a bachelor's degree. However, most new agents have an advanced degree, such as a master's or juris doctorate. After being hired, all new agents undergo 16 weeks of training at the FBI Academy in Quantico, Virginia.

Q. What are some of the pros and cons of work as an FBI agent?

A. The biggest negative is the frequent work required at nights and on weekends, along with the unpredictable nature of the job. FBI agents are on call 24 hours a day and are often called out with little or no notice. The biggest positive is the sense of accomplishment that comes with the successful resolution of a case.

Q. What advice would you give to high school students who are interested in this field?

A. Explore as many career opportunities as possible, taking advantage of the many resources that are now available to students planning for college and careers. The ability to communicate effectively, especially to read and write, is probably the single most important skill that a person can have in being an FBI agent.

Federal and State Officials

OVERVIEW

Federal and state officials hold positions in the legislative, executive, and judicial branches of government at the state and national levels. They include governors, judges, senators, representatives, and the president and vice president of the country. Government officials are responsible for preserving the government against external and domestic threats, supervising and resolving conflicts between private and public interest, regulating the economy, protecting political and social rights of the citizens, and providing goods and services. Officials may, among other things, pass laws, set up social service programs, and allocate taxpayers' money on goods and services.

HISTORY

In ancient states, the scope of government was almost without limitation. As Aristotle put it, "What was not commanded by the government was forbidden." Government functions were challenged by Christianity during the Roman Empire, when the enforcement of religious sanctions became the focus of political authority. It was not until the 18th century that the modern concept of government as separate from the church came into being.

The Roman Republic had a great deal of influence on those who framed the U.S. Constitution. The supreme council of state in ancient Rome was called the "Senate." Even the name "Capitol Hill" is derived from "Capitoline Hill" of Rome. The Congress of the United States was modeled after British

Parliament and assumed the powers that London had held before American independence. Limiting the powers of the individual states, the U.S. Congress was empowered to levy taxes, engage in foreign diplomacy, and regulate Native American affairs.

THE JOB

Think about the last time you cast a vote, whether in a school, local, state, or federal election. How did you make your decision? Was it based on the personal qualities of the candidate? The political positions of the candidate? Certain issues of importance to you? Or do you always vote for the same political party? As voters, we choose carefully when electing a government official, taking many different things into consideration. Whether you're electing a new governor and lieutenant governor for the state, a president and vice president for the country, or senators and representatives for the state legislature or the U.S. Congress, you're choosing people to act on behalf of your interests. The decisions of state and federal lawmakers affect your daily life and your future. State and federal officials pass laws concerning the arts, education, taxes, employment, health care, and other areas, in efforts to change and improve communities and standards of living.

Besides the *president* and *vice president* of the United States, the executive branch of the national government consists of the president's Cabinet, including, among others, the secretaries of state, treasury, defense, interior, agriculture, homeland security, and health and human services. These officials are appointed by the president and approved by the Senate. The members of the Office of Management and Budget, the Council of Economic Advisers, and the National Security Council are also executive officers of the national government.

Nearly every state's governing body resembles that of the federal government. Just as the U.S. Congress is composed of the Senate and the House of Representatives, so does each state (with one exception, Nebraska) have a senate and a house. The executive branch of the U.S. government is headed by the president and vice president, while the states elect governors and lieutenant governors. The *governor* is the chief executive officer of a state. In all states, a large government administration handles a variety of functions related to agriculture, highway and motor vehicle supervision, public safety and corrections, regulation of intrastate business and industry, and some aspects of education, public health, and welfare. The governor's job is to manage this administration. Some states also have a *lieutenant governor,* who serves as the presiding officer of the state's senate. Other elected officials commonly include a secretary of state, state treasurer, state auditor, attorney general, and superintendent of public instruction.

State senators and *state representatives* are the legislators elected to represent the districts and regions of cities and counties within the state. The number of members of a state's legislature varies from state to state. In the U.S. Congress, there are 100 senators (as established by the Constitution—two senators from each state) and 435 representatives. The number of representatives each state is allowed to send to the U.S. Congress varies based on the state's population as determined by the national census. Based on results from Census 2000, California is the most populous state and sends the most representatives (53). The primary function of all legislators, on both the state and national levels, is to make laws. With a staff of aides, senators and representatives attempt to learn as much as they can about the bills being considered. They research legislation, prepare reports, meet with constituents and interest groups, speak to the press, and discuss and debate legislation on the floor of the House or Senate. Legislators also may be involved in selecting other members of the government, supervising the government administration, appropriating funds, impeaching executive and judicial officials, and determining election procedures, among other activities. A state legislator may be involved in examining such situations as the state's relationship to Native American tribes, the level of school violence, and welfare reform.

"Time in each day goes by so quickly," says Don Preister, who serves on the state legislature in Nebraska, "there's no time to read up on all legislation and all the information the constituents send in." The state of Nebraska is the only state with a single-house system. When the state senate is in session, Preister commits many hours to discussing and debating issues with other state senators and gathering information on proposed legislation. In addition to senate sessions, Preister attends committee hearings. His committees include Natural Resources and Urban Affairs. "A hearing lasts from 20 minutes to three or four hours," he says, "depending on the intensity of the issues." Despite having to devote about 60 hours a week to the job when the Senate is in session, Preister finds his work a wonderful opportunity to be of service to the community and to improve lives. "I take a lot of personal satisfaction from being a voice for people whose voices aren't often heard in government."

REQUIREMENTS

High School

Courses in government, civics, and history will give you an understanding of the structure of state and federal governments. English

Did You Know?

- 7,382 elected members serve in state legislatures in the United States.
- The largest legislature is found in New Hampshire (400 seats, House of Representatives); the smallest is in Alaska (20 seats, Senate).
- Fifteen states have set term limits for their legislators.
- Women hold 22.6 percent of seats in state legislatures—approximately 60 percent of female legislators are Democrats
- Only 8.1 percent of legislators are African American and only 2.9 percent are Hispanic American—percentages that are significantly lower than their representation in the total U.S. population.
- Lawyers make up the largest (15 percent) occupational group of legislators.
- The average age of state legislators is 53.

Source: National Conference of State Legislatures

courses are important because you need good writing skills for communicating with constituents and other government officials. Math and accounting help you to develop the analytical skills needed for examining statistics and demographics. You should take science courses because you'll be making decisions concerning health, medicine, and technological advances. Journalism classes will help you learn about the print and broadcast media and the role they play in politics. Take public speaking courses, as communicating verbally is fundamental to a career as a public official.

Postsecondary Training
State and federal legislators come from all walks of life. Some hold master's degrees and doctorates, while others have only a high school education. Although a majority of government officials hold law degrees, others have undergraduate or graduate degrees in such areas as journalism, economics, political science, history, and English. Regardless of your major as an undergraduate, it is important to take classes in English literature, statistics, foreign language, Western civilization, and economics. Graduate studies can focus more on one area of study; some prospective government officials pursue master's degrees in public administration or international affairs. Consider participating in an internship program that will involve you with local and state officials. Contact the offices of your state legislators and of your state's members of Congress to apply for internships directly.

President George W. Bush thanks Department of Homeland Security employees for their contributions to the fight against terrorism. *(U.S. Customs and Border Protection)*

Other Requirements

"You should have concern for people," Don Preister says. "You should have an ability to listen and understand people and their concerns." This attention to the needs of communities should be of foremost importance to anyone pursuing a government office. Although historically some politicians have had questionable purposes in their campaigns for office, most successful politicians are devoted to making positive changes and improvements. Good people skills will help you make connections, get elected, and make things happen once in office. You should also enjoy public speaking, argument, debate, and opposition—you'll get a lot of it as you attempt to get laws passed. A good temperament in such situations will earn you the respect of your colleagues. Strong character and a good background will help you to avoid the personal attacks that occasionally accompany government office.

EXPLORING

If you are 16 or older, you can gain experience in a legislature. The U.S. Congress and possibly your state legislature offer opportunities for young adults who have demonstrated a commitment to government study to work as *pages*. For Congress, pages run messages across Capitol Hill and have the opportunity to see senators and representatives debating and discussing bills. The length of a page's service can be for one summer or up to one year. Contact your state's senator or representative for an application.

You can also explore government careers by becoming involved with local elections. Many candidates for local and state offices welcome young people to assist with campaigns. You might be asked to make calls, post signs, or hand out information about the candidate. Not only will you get to see the politician at work, but you will also meet others with an interest in government.

Another great way to learn about government is to become involved in an issue of interest to you. Participate with a grassroots advocacy group or read about the bills up for vote in the state legislature and U.S. Congress. When you feel strongly about an issue and are well educated on the subject, contact the offices of state legislators and members of Congress to express your views. Visit the Web sites of the House and Senate and of your state legislature to read about bills, schedules, and the legislators. The National Conference of State Legislators (NCSL) also hosts a Web site (http://www.ncsl. org) featuring legislative news and links to state legislatures.

EMPLOYERS

State legislators work for the state government, and many hold other jobs as well. Because of the part-time nature of some legislative offices, state legislators may hold part-time jobs or own their own businesses. Federal officials work full time for the Senate, the House, or the executive branch.

STARTING OUT

There is no direct career path for state and federal officials. Some enter into their positions after some success with political activism on the grassroots level. Others work their way up from local government positions to state legislature and into federal office. Those who serve as U.S. Congress members have worked in the military, journalism, academics, business, and many other fields.

Many politicians get their start assisting someone else's campaign or advocating for an issue. Don Preister's beginnings with the Nebraska state legislature are particularly inspiring. Because of his involvement in grassroots organizing to improve his neighborhood, he was encouraged by friends and neighbors to run for senator of the district. Others, however, believed he'd never get elected running against a man who'd had a lot of political success, as well as great finances to back his campaign. "I didn't have any money," Preister says, "or any experience in campaigning. So I went door to door to meet the people of the district. I went to every house and apartment in the district." He won that election in 1992 and won again in 1996, 2000, and 2004.

ADVANCEMENT

Initiative is one key to success in politics. Advancement can be rapid for someone who is a fast learner and is independently motivated, but a career in politics most often takes a long time to establish. Most state and federal officials start by pursuing training and work experience in their particular field, while getting involved in politics at the local level. Many people progress from local politics to state politics. It is not uncommon for a state legislator to eventually run for a seat in Congress. Appointees to the president's Cabinet and presidential and vice presidential candidates frequently have held positions in Congress.

EARNINGS

In general, salaries for government officials tend to be lower than what the official could make working in the private sector. In the case of state legislators, the pay can be very much lower.

The U.S. Department of Labor reports that government legislators earned median annual salaries of $18,500 in 2004. Salaries generally ranged from less than $11,920 to more than $72,780, although some officials earn nothing at all.

According to the NCSL, state legislators make from $10,000 (Mississippi) to $110,880 (California) a year. A few states, however, don't pay state legislators anything but an expense allowance. Salaries of state governors are typically much higher.

U.S. senators and representatives earned $165,200 in 2006; the vice president was paid $205,031 in 2005; and the president earned $400,000 in 2005.

Congressional leaders receive higher salaries than the other Congress members. For example, the Senate Majority and Minority leaders and the President Pro Tempore earned $180,100 in 2006. U.S. Congress members receive excellent insurance, vacation, and other benefits.

WORK ENVIRONMENT

Most government officials work in a typical office setting. Some may work a regular 40-hour week, while others typically work long hours and weekends. One potential drawback to political life, particularly for the candidate running for office, is that there is no real off-duty time. One is continually under observation by the press and public, and the personal lives of candidates and officeholders are discussed frequently in the media.

Because these officials must be appointed or elected in order to keep their jobs, the ability to determine long-range job objectives is slim. There may be extended periods of unemployment, when living off of savings or working at other jobs may be necessary.

Frequent travel is involved in campaigning and in holding office, so some people with children may find the lifestyle demanding on their families.

OUTLOOK

The U.S. Department of Labor predicts that employment of federal and state officials will grow about as fast as the average through 2014. To attract more candidates to run for legislative offices, states may consider salary increases and better benefits for state senators and representatives. But changes in pay and benefits for federal officials are unlikely. An increase in the number of representatives is possible as the U.S. population grows, but would require additional office space and other costly expansions. For the most part, the structures of state and federal legislatures will remain unchanged, although the topic of limiting the number of terms that a representative is allowed to serve does often arise in election years.

The federal government has made efforts to shift costs to the states; if this continues, it could change the way state legislatures and executive officers operate with regard to public funding. Already, welfare reform has resulted in state governments looking for financial aid in handling welfare cases and job programs. Arts funding may also become the sole responsibility of the states as programs such as the National Endowment for the Arts lose support from Congress.

With the government's commitment to developing a place on the Internet, contacting your state and federal representatives, learning about legislation, and organizing grassroots advocacy have become much easier. This voter awareness of candidates, public policy issues, and legislation will increase and may affect how future representatives make decisions. Also look for government programming to be part of cable television's expansion into digital broadcasting. New modes of communication will allow constituents to become even more involved in the actions of their representatives.

FOR MORE INFORMATION

For more information about House and Senate employment studies and other publications, such as the Congressional Intern Handbook, contact
Congressional Management Foundation
513 Capitol Court, NE, Suite 300
Washington, DC 20002-7709
Tel: 202-546-0100
Email: cmf@cmfweb.org
http://www.cmfweb.org

To purchase publications about state government, contact
Council of State Governments
PO Box 11910
2760 Research Park Drive
Lexington, KY 40578-1910
Tel: 859-244-8000
http://www.statesnews.org

*To read about state legislatures, policy issues, legislative news, and
other related information, visit the NCSL's Web site:*
**National Conference of State Legislatures
    (NCSL)**
444 North Capitol Street, NW, Suite 515
Washington, DC 20001-1512
Tel: 202-624-5400
Email: info@ncsl.org
http://www.ncsl.org

For information on state governors, contact
National Governors Association
Hall of the States
444 North Capitol Street, Suite 267
Washington, DC 20001-1512
Tel: 202-624-5300
http://www.nga.org

*Visit the Senate and House Web sites for extensive information
about Congress, government history, current legislation, and links
to state legislature sites. To inquire about internship opportunities
with your Congress member, contact*
U.S. Senate
Office of Senator (Name)
Washington, DC 20510
http://www.senate.gov

U.S. House of Representatives
Office of the Honorable (Name)
Washington, DC 20510
http://www.house.gov

Federal Aviation Security Workers

OVERVIEW

Federal aviation security worker is a blanket term describing people in several jobs—such as security screeners and air marshals—who protect the safety of passengers and staff in the nation's airports and aircraft. One of the largest groups of personnel in this line of work is *security screeners,* who are responsible for identifying dangerous objects or hazardous materials in baggage, cargo, or on traveling passengers and preventing these objects and their carriers from boarding planes. Also included in this group of workers are *air marshals,* who act as onboard security agents, protecting passengers, pilots, and other airline staff in case of any emergencies while in the air. There are approximately 43,000 security screeners working in the nation's airports; the number of air marshals and aviation security directors is classified.

HISTORY

The use of screening and onboard security personnel is not a recent invention. The presence of guards on airplanes originated in the 1960s as a result of a number of hijackings of U.S. planes flying to and from Cuba. These guards, referred to as sky marshals, grew in number during the 1970s and then declined in later years with the lower occurrences of airplane hijackings. Airplane security staffing reached several thousand workers at the peak of this hijacking scare and dropped to fewer than 100 workers nationwide during its quietest times.

QUICK FACTS

School Subjects
Computer science
Government
Mathematics

Personal Skills
Following instructions
Leadership/management

Work Environment
Indoors and outdoors
Primarily multiple locations

Minimum Education Level
Some postsecondary training

Salary Range
$23,000 to $35,000 to $150,000+

Certification or Licensing
None available

Outlook
Faster than the average

DOT
372

GOE
04.02.02

NOC
6651

O*NET-SOC
33-9032.00

The 2001 terrorist attacks on the World Trade Center and the Pentagon spurred many changes in the realm of airport security. Most notably, a new federal agency was born: The Transportation Security Administration (TSA), responsible for overseeing all security at the nation's airports. This agency made airport and airline security a federal responsibility. As a result, all airport security personnel became federal employees. This was no small task. Previously, security screening in airports was handled by private security firms. These firms were inconsistent in their hiring and training methods and paid relatively low wages—resulting in high job turnover rates and inadequate screening of potentially dangerous objects and materials. With the shift of responsibility into the government's hands, standard training and hiring requirements were put in place. In addition to better screening, hiring, and training methods, the technology for screening bags and passengers has improved, increasing the chances that dangerous cargo and on-person threats can be located and prevented from boarding a plane.

THE JOB

Protecting U.S. skies, airports, and passengers is a huge undertaking that requires many well-trained individuals in different security roles. The most visible federal aviation security worker is the *security screener,* also called the *baggage and passenger screener.* These workers are responsible for identifying dangerous objects or hazardous materials in baggage, cargo, or on traveling passengers and preventing these objects and their carriers from boarding planes. They use computers, X-ray machines, and handheld scanners to screen bags and their owners passing through airport terminals. In addition to using technology to help them identify dangerous items, they have to depend on their own eyesight to catch suspicious behavior and read the X-ray screens for signs of danger. These workers must be focused and alert, while also remaining personable and courteous to people being screened. The screening process can take a lot of time during high-volume travel days, and passengers waiting in line may be late for a flight, impatient, or simply rude. For this reason, security screeners must be people oriented, able to manage crowds, and able to maintain composure in what can be stressful conditions.

The need for security is not limited to the ground. *Air marshals* have the demanding job of protecting all airline passengers and staff from on-board threats such as terrorists, hijackers, bombs, or other weapons. These workers are often covert in their operations, meaning they may be dressed and seated like an average passenger to be able to watch for suspicious behavior and surprise a potential attacker. Many of the details of air marshal jobs are classified to protect national security, such as their exact number and identities, routes, and training procedures. However, the aim of their job is much like that of a Secret Service agent. They must be attentive to all activity that goes on around them, identify potential threats to security, and deal with dangerous individuals or objects once exposed on board. The main difference between air marshals and other types of federal aviation security workers is that air marshals must be trained and able to handle possible warfare in a confined space at 30,000 feet in the air or above.

Another federal aviation security job of high importance is that of *aviation security director*. These workers, hired by the federal government, are responsible for all security personnel within an airport. They oversee the hiring, training, and work of baggage and passenger screeners and other security guards. In the nation's largest airports, such as LaGuardia (in New York City) or O'Hare (in Chicago), directors are in charge of hundreds of workers. Because of the high level of responsibility these workers hold, federal security directors often have experience in crisis management or law enforcement, such as police chiefs or military officers.

REQUIREMENTS

High School
To work in most federal aviation security jobs, you should have at least a high school diploma. However, security screeners can sidestep this educational requirement with job experience in security. While in high school, take classes in history and government to familiarize yourself with events and political threats that have threatened our national security, such as foreign hijackers and terrorist operations. You should also be comfortable working with computers, since most jobs in security involve a great deal of technology. Math classes can be beneficial; as a security worker, you must be analytical and observant to identify and catch dangers before they happen. If you plan to become an air marshal, take as many physical education classes as you can. It is also a good idea to take government, history, criminal justice, and psychology classes. Aspiring security directors should take government, history, criminal justice, mathematics, and psychology classes.

Postsecondary Training
Screeners and air marshals are highly trained before starting their jobs. Screeners are trained on how to operate and identify dangerous

objects using X-ray machines and handheld wands. They also must be prepared to manage potentially dangerous individuals. Screeners currently receive 40 hours of training before their first day at work and an additional 60 hours of training while on the job. This training period may be extended due to increased scrutiny on screeners' performance and heightened national security risks.

Air marshals are rigorously trained in classified training centers across the country and come to the job with on-the-job experience, having served in a military or civilian police force.

Aviation security directors do not receive much on-the-job training, because these individuals are already at the top of their profession and have years of training and experience in the field when they are hired.

Other Requirements

All federal aviation security personnel have demanding jobs that require a calm demeanor when under pressure. Screeners often have to stand for hours at a time and assist in lifting passengers' luggage onto the screening belt. Screeners' eyesight must be strong enough to detect even the smallest of possible threats displayed on a computer screen. To ensure that individuals can handle these demands, potential screeners face many physical and vision tests to ensure they are up to the job. As of November 2001, all screeners must be U.S. citizens or nationals and pass tests evaluating mental abilities (English reading, writing, and speaking), visual observation (including color perception), sense of hearing, and manual dexterity. Similarly, air marshals must pass vision and hearing tests and be in good physical shape to face and dominate potential attackers.

Aviation security directors must have strong management and communication skills. In addition, they must be analytical and possess comprehensive knowledge of security procedures and practices.

EXPLORING

To explore this job, watch people at work the next time you are at the airport. Notice how many people are involved in screening luggage and passengers. Although you should not talk to these screeners and other security staff while they are at work, you may be able to schedule an interview with security personnel while they are on break or perhaps over the phone. Talk to a teacher or your school's guidance counselor for help in arranging this.

You can also learn about security jobs at your local library or online. Explore the Web site of the Federal Aviation Administration (FAA) for facts and job descriptions, changes in policy, and even

Books to Read

Bullock, Jane A., et. al. *Introduction to Homeland Security*. Burlington, Mass.: Butterworth-Heinemann, 2004.

Hutton, Donald B., and Anna Mydlarz. *Guide to Homeland Security Careers*. Hauppauge, N.Y.: Barrons Educational Series, 2003.

Peat, Barbara. *From College to Career: A Guide For Criminal Justice Majors*. Boston: Allyn and Bacon, 2004.

Stephens, W. Richard, Jr. *Careers in Criminal Justice*. Boston: Allyn and Bacon, 2002.

White, Jonathan R. *Terrorism: An Introduction*. Belmont, Calif.: Wadsworth Publishing, 2002.

summer camp opportunities. The links at the end of this article are good places to start your research.

EMPLOYERS

In late 2001, airport and airline security was placed under the oversight of the federal government. While some screening jobs may still be handled by private companies, all security personnel are screened and trained under federal rules and regulations. This shift in responsibility occurred to improve standards in security and ensure the safety of U.S. passengers and airline staff. The newly created Transportation Security Administration employs all security screeners, air marshals, and aviation security directors. Approximately 43,000 security screeners work in the nation's airports; the number of air marshals and aviation security directors is classified.

STARTING OUT

Depending on the security capacity you want to be employed in, you can start out working with no more than a high school diploma and on-the-job training. Security screening jobs are a great way to start out in this line of work. These jobs provide front-line experience in airport security and can offer flexible part-time schedules.

Positions as air marshals or directors of security are not entry level. If you are interested in one of these jobs, you will need experience with the police, U.S. military, or other organization in which you have gained skills in protecting the lives of others.

ADVANCEMENT

Screening jobs have high turnover rates. As a result, they offer many chances for advancement. After a couple of years of experience in baggage and passenger screening, you can work into higher positions in management or busier traffic responsibility. Aviation security directors may be responsible for hundreds of workers and oversee the hiring and training of new workers.

Positions as air marshals already carry high levels of responsibility, but qualified and talented individuals can advance into manager and director roles, responsible for hundreds and even thousands of workers.

EARNINGS

Before airline security was adopted by the Transportation Security Administration, screeners were paid minimum wage. But to attract and retain qualified and dedicated workers, earnings have been increased considerably, with most full-time screeners earning salaries of $23,000 to $35,000 a year. Their pay increases as their level of experience and responsibility increases. Air marshals and directors earn much more, with aviation security directors topping out at a salary of $150,000 or more—one of the highest salaries in government service.

WORK ENVIRONMENT

As previously stated, any job in airport security is demanding and stressful, especially during high periods of travel such as the holidays. Screeners face physical challenges of standing, bending, and lifting during their shifts, while the having to maintain total visual focus on their X-ray machines or while searching individual passengers by hand.

The job of air marshals can be extremely stressful. These workers must be prepared to overcome an attacker in a confined space without risking harm to any of the plane's passengers. In addition, air marshals must spend considerable time away from home.

OUTLOOK

With the new awareness of airline dangers following the 2001 terrorist attacks, the employment of aviation security workers will grow at a faster-than-average rate. Despite better pay, security screeners still have high turnover rates due to the high demands involved with the job. This turnover will continue to create many new jobs in the future. While jobs as air marshals and aviation security directors will not be as plentiful, there will always be a critical need for qualified and skilled individuals to protect airplanes and passengers from security threats.

FOR MORE INFORMATION

The FAA offers a wealth of information on its Web site, from airline accident statistics to career guidance. Visit the Education & Research page for information on summer camps for middle and high school students interested in aviation careers.

Federal Aviation Administration (FAA)
800 Independence Avenue, SW
Washington, DC 20591-0001
Tel: 866-835-5322
http://www.faa.gov

According to its Web site, the TSA "sets the standard for excellence in transportation security through its people, processes, and technologies." Explore the site for details on the nation's threat advisory level and tips on flying and packing safely.

Transportation Security Administration (TSA)
601 South 12th Street
Arlington, VA 22202-4220
http://www.tsa.gov

Fish and Game Wardens

QUICK FACTS

School Subjects
Biology
Earth science

Personal Skills
Helping/teaching
Leadership/management

Work Environment
Primarily outdoors
Primarily multiple locations

Minimum Education Level
Bachelor's degree

Salary Range
$18,000 to $31,209 to
$91,000

Certification or Licensing
Required for certain positions

Outlook
About as fast as the average

DOT
379

GOE
04.01.02

NOC
2224

O*NET-SOC
33-3031.00

OVERVIEW

Professional wildlife conservationists, once widely known as *fish and game wardens,* are now known by a variety of titles. Jobs falling under this category in the federal government include *U.S. Fish and Wildlife Service special agents, federal law enforcement officers, wildlife inspectors, refuge rangers,* and *refuge officers.* On a state or municipal level, the job title might be *conservation police, environmental conservation police,* or *conservation wardens.* Along with the job title, the job itself has expanded. Once, the fish and game wardens were hired solely to protect wildlife. Today, in addition to that original purpose, they perform a wide variety of tasks related to resource management, public information, and law enforcement. More than 7,500 people are employed by the U.S. Fish and Wildlife Service.

HISTORY

For centuries, wildlife has suffered because of the actions of human beings. Increasingly efficient weaponry—bows, rifles, shotguns—made it easier for people to kill game. ("Game" may be broadly defined as any fish, birds, or mammals hunted noncommercially for food, sport, or both.) Some species of animals have been hunted to extinction. Forests have been cleared, swamps drained, and rivers dammed to clear the way for agriculture and industry. These activities have harmed or destroyed large areas of plant and wildlife habitat.

Beginning in the late 19th century, growing concern for vanishing wildlife led to the initiation of comprehensive conservation actions. The governments of the United States and other nations have since passed protective laws and set aside national parks and other reserves for wildlife.

The principal agency assigned to the conservation and enhancement of animals and their habitats in this country is the U.S. Fish and Wildlife Service. An agency of the U.S. Department of the Interior, it is responsible for the scientific development of commercial fisheries and the conservation of fish and wildlife. The service, which was created in 1856, manages the 95 million-acre National Wildlife Refuge System. This system includes more than 535 National Wildlife Refuges, thousands of smaller wetlands, and other special-management areas. It also operates 69 National Fish Hatcheries, 64 fishery resource offices, nine Fish Health Centers, seven Fish Technology Centers, and 78 ecological services field stations.

THE JOB

The conservation of fish and wildlife is a responsibility that grows more complex each year, especially with growing pollution and environmental changes. To accomplish its mission, the U.S. Fish and Wildlife Service, for example, employs many of the country's best biologists, wildlife managers, engineers, realty specialists, law enforcement agents, and others who work to save endangered and threatened species; conserve migratory birds and inland fisheries; provide expert advice to other federal agencies, industry, and foreign governments; and manage nearly 700 offices and field stations. These personnel work in every state and territory from the Arctic Ocean to the South Pacific and from the Atlantic to the Caribbean.

Wildlife inspectors and *special agents* are two job titles that have arisen from "fish and game wardens." Wildlife inspectors monitor the legal trade and intercept illegal importations and exportations of federally protected fish and wildlife. At points of entry into the United States, wildlife inspectors examine shipping containers, live animals, wildlife products such as animal skins, and documents. Inspectors, who work closely with special agents, may seize shipments as evidence, conduct investigations, and testify in courts of law.

Special agents of the U.S. Fish and Wildlife Service are trained criminal investigators who enforce federal wildlife laws throughout this country. Special agents conduct law enforcement investigations, which may include activities such as surveillance, undercover work, making arrests, and preparing cases for court. They often work with other federal, tribal, foreign, state, or local law enforcement authorities. These agents enforce traditional migratory bird regulations and investigate commercial activities involving illegal trade in protected wildlife. Some agents work at border ports to enforce federal laws protecting wildlife that enters interstate and national commerce.

Another prominent position within the Fish and Wildlife Service is that of a *refuge ranger* or *refuge manager.* These professionals work at more than 535 national refuges across the country, protecting and conserving migratory and native species of birds, mammals, fish, endangered species, and other wildlife. Many of these refuges also offer outdoor recreational opportunities and programs to educate the public about the refuges' wildlife and their habitats.

Judie Miller is a refuge ranger and public affairs officer at the Minnesota Valley National Wildlife Refuge, located in Bloomington, Minnesota. She is responsible for outreach at the refuge, "which means that I need to inform not only the public, but our internal audiences, about our mission and what we are doing."

Miller notes that "refuge ranger" is a pretty generic title. "Some of our rangers work in law enforcement; some are environmental educators and interpreters; some work in public affairs or as volunteer officers. These are some of the functional jobs within the generic category. My job also includes handling a number of special events at Minnesota Valley. For example, I coordinate the National Wildlife Refuge Week events at this refuge. I do many other outreach jobs—such as creating and writing newsletters, press releases, etc., to get word out to people about our refuge."

The U.S Fish and Wildlife Service also employs people in a wide variety of occupations such as engineering; ecology; zoology; veterinary science; forestry; botany; chemistry; hydrology; land surveying; architecture; landscape architecture; statistics; library science; archaeology; education; and guidance counseling. The service hires administrators and business managers; realty specialists; appraisers; assessors; contract specialists; purchasing agents; budget analysts; financial managers; computer specialists and programmers; human resources professionals; and public affairs specialists. Additionally, a variety of technical, clerical, and trades and crafts positions are available.

REQUIREMENTS
High School
It is advisable for high school students interested in a career in this field to take courses in biology and other science subjects, geography,

mathematics, social studies, and physical education. Judie Miller recommends that you look for cooperative programs available at some high schools and colleges; these programs allow you to study as well as work in programs at refuges and other facilities—and, in some cases, get paid for some of the hours you work at the facility.

Postsecondary Training
All positions in this category require a bachelor's degree or three years of work-related experience. Higher positions require at least one year of graduate studies; as you move up the scale to increasingly professional positions, master's or even doctoral degrees become mandatory.

Specialized positions require advanced education or training. For example, all biology-related positions require a bachelor's degree in biology or natural resources management or a combination of education and experience equivalent to a degree that includes an appropriate number of semester hours in biological science. Visit http://www.fws.gov/hr/HR/Careers_FWS.htm for an overview of educational requirements for various positions in the service.

Additional on-the-job training is given for most positions. Natural-resource managers and related professionals receive training at the National Conservation Training Center in Shepherdstown, WV. Special agents are given 18 weeks of formal training in criminal investigative and wildlife law enforcement techniques at the Federal Law Enforcement Training Center in Glynco, Georgia. In addition, the service typically requires its employees to receive 40 hours of training each year.

Other Requirements
Some positions have physical fitness and ability requirements, so you must undergo a battery of physical tests. To qualify for a special agent position, you must meet strict medical, physical, and psychological requirements. You must also participate in mandatory drug testing and psychological screening programs.

Only the most highly qualified candidates will be interviewed for special agent positions. Those chosen undergo extensive background investigations to determine suitability for appointment. All special agent appointees must be citizens of the United States and between 21 and 37 years of age when entering. Additionally, you must sign a mobility agreement, which indicates a willingness to accept a reassignment to any location in the future.

It is important to bear in mind that fish and game wardens don't just work with fish and game. They spend a lot of time working with other officials and with members of the general public. Therefore, they must have good communication skills and enjoy working with people as much as caring for animals.

EXPLORING

Doing volunteer work at a fish and wildlife facility is a good way to get some experience in this field and to determine whether you would like to pursue a career in the area. Of course, it would be ideal to volunteer for the U.S. Fish and Wildlife Service, but serving with other environmental organizations can be very useful as well. College students—and even students at select high schools—can apply for formal internships with various wildlife agencies. These can usually provide college (or possibly high school) credit and may even pay a small stipend.

EMPLOYERS

The largest number of jobs in the field is found with the U.S. Fish and Wildlife Service and other agencies of the Department of the Interior—such as the National Park Service. Individual states also have positions in this area; contact your local state government, especially the state's park association. In Illinois, for example, you might contact the Illinois Department of Natural Resources.

STARTING OUT

The U.S. Fish and Wildlife Service fills jobs in various ways, including promoting or reassigning current employees, transferring employees from other federal agencies, rehiring former federal employees, or hiring applicants from outside the federal service. Some summer jobs are also filled by hiring applicants. Applications for these positions must be submitted during a specified period—usually sometime between January and April of each year. The number and types of temporary positions vary from year to year. Contact the regional office nearest you to learn about current opportunities.

For information about specific Fish and Wildlife Service job openings, contact the Office of Personnel Management Area Office. Your telephone directory will list the number and address of the office nearest you (under U.S. Government). Career planning and placement directors at colleges and universities can supply career information and training opportunities. Also, state employment or job services offices maintain listings of federal position vacancies. These offices can help you obtain the necessary forms to apply for jobs or direct you to sources for additional information.

A great way to check job listings is over the Internet, where you can access USAJOBS (http://www.usajobs.opm.gov), a job bank for the U.S. government.

ADVANCEMENT

Prospects for advancement in this field improve greatly if fish and game wardens are willing to relocate. While they certainly can be promoted within their own facility, relocation opens up the possibility of taking a higher position whenever one opens at any U.S. Fish and Wildlife Service location around the country.

EARNINGS

Like all federal employees, those who work for the U.S. Fish and Wildlife Service earn salaries as prescribed by law. Service employees are classified either as "general schedule" (GS) or as "wage grade" (WG). General schedule employees, the professional, technical, administrative, and clerical workers, receive annual salaries based on their GS grades 1 through 15. GS-5 salaries in 2006 ranged from $25,195 to $32,755. GS-7 salaries ranged from $31,209 to $40,569. GS-9 salaries ranged from $38,175 to $49,632. There are some areas in the U.S. that have an additional geographic locality pay.

In the wide variety of positions available at the U.S. Fish and Wildlife Service, salaries range from $18,000 all the way up to $91,000 for more advanced positions. Law enforcement positions, especially special agents, receive higher salaries because of the danger inherent in their jobs.

WORK ENVIRONMENT

With a number of different positions available, the work environment for each, of course, varies substantially. Wildlife inspectors, conservation police, or special agents generally spend a great deal of time outdoors, sometimes in remote areas, perhaps pursuing wildlife criminals. Yet they also need to spend time indoors, preparing detailed reports of their investigations and seeking additional information by searching on their computers.

A refuge ranger or manager will divide his or her work time between indoor and outdoor activities. The various types of biologists will also spend time both indoors and outdoors, as their particular job dictates. All of these employees, however, will have a passion for the land and animal life, a dedication to preserving our environment, and the desire to make a difference in effecting positive changes. It can be very rewarding work in terms of personal satisfaction and sense of accomplishment. Very few of these jobs are of the nine-to-five variety, though; most require putting in extra hours.

OUTLOOK

As with any career with the government, the potential for growth depends a lot on the political climate and what the views are of those in power, whether on a national or local level. However, as Judie Miller says, there is "lots of work to be done and people are becoming more and more concerned about environmental issues. We need to have good water, good places to play and swim and hunt and fish. Jobs are always available, but the number depends on the political situation at a given time."

FOR MORE INFORMATION

To learn more about fish and game wardens and related employment opportunities, contact the following organizations
U.S. Fish and Wildlife Service
Department of the Interior
1849 C Street, NW
Washington, DC 20240-0001
Tel: 800-344-WILD
http://www.fws.gov

U.S. National Park Service
Department of the Interior
1849 C Street, NW
Washington, DC 20240-0001
Tel: 202-208-6843
http://www.nps.gov

Foreign
Service Officers

OVERVIEW

Foreign Service officers represent the government and the people of the United States by conducting relations with foreign countries and international organizations. They promote and protect the United States' political, economic, and commercial interests overseas. They observe and analyze conditions and developments in foreign countries and report to the State Department and other agencies. Foreign Service officers guard the welfare of Americans abroad and help foreign nationals traveling to the United States. There are about 9,000 Foreign Service employees in the nearly 265 U.S. embassies and consulates and in Washington, D.C.

HISTORY

The Foreign Service is a branch of the U.S. Department of State, which plans and carries out U.S. foreign policy under the authority of the president. Established in 1789, the State Department was placed under the direction of Thomas Jefferson, the first U.S. secretary of state and the senior officer in President George Washington's cabinet. It was his responsibility to initiate foreign policy on behalf of the U.S. government, advise the president on matters related to foreign policy, and administer the foreign affairs of the United States with the help of employees both at home and abroad.

The Foreign Service wasn't actually established until 1924, when the Diplomatic and Consular Services were brought together as one organization. The Foreign Service was formed in anticipation of a trade war; security issues became the service's focus with World

QUICK FACTS

School Subjects
Foreign language
Government
History

Personal Skills
Communication/ideas
Leadership/management

Work Environment
Primarily indoors
Primarily multiple locations

Minimum Education Level
Bachelor's degree

Salary Range
$39,961 to $50,000 to
$100,000+

Certification or Licensing
None available

Outlook
About as fast as the average

DOT
188

GOE
N/A

NOC
4168

O*NET-SOC
N/A

War II and remained so throughout the Cold War. With the end of the Cold War, issues such as trade protection and combating terrorism have come to the forefront of the service's concerns. Other foreign policy issues facing today's Foreign Service officers include the global struggle to eliminate diseases such as AIDS, efforts to protect the environment, and international law enforcement regarding drug trafficking and science and technology issues.

THE JOB

Foreign Service officers work in embassies and consulates throughout the world. Between foreign assignments, they may have duties in the Department of State in Washington, D.C., or they may be temporarily detailed to the Department of Defense, the Department of Commerce, or other government departments and agencies. Similarly, Foreign Service information officers serve abroad or may work in the Office of International Information headquarters in Washington, D.C.

James Prosser spent 36 years with the Foreign Service. Though he is retired, he visits academic and civic organizations to lecture about the history of the Foreign Service. As an officer, Prosser worked in the telecommunications and computer fields as an operator, engineer, manager, and international negotiator. He speaks German, French, and Italian. Among his experiences: In what was then Belgian Congo, he ran a communications center and shortwave radio station during the country's postcolonial struggle for independence, a time when many were losing their lives in the upheaval; in 1967, France expelled the North Atlantic Treaty Organization (NATO) headquarters and Prosser was placed in charge of moving the U.S. communications elements of NATO to Belgium, as well as designing the new communications facilities there. Prosser has served in Germany, Italy, Kenya, and other countries. "Being in charge of all U.S. government telecommunications facilities in Africa and the Indian Ocean was an especially gratifying challenge," Prosser says. He still visits Africa whenever possible. The work of Foreign Service officers is divided into five broad areas: Management Affairs, Consular Affairs, Economic Affairs, Political Affairs, and Public Diplomacy.

Management officers who work in embassies and consulates manage and administer the day-to-day operations of their posts. Some handle financial matters such as planning budgets and controlling expenditures. Others work in general services: They purchase and look after government property and supplies, negotiate leases and contracts for office space and housing, and make arrangements for travel and shipping. *Personnel officers* deal with assignments, promotions, and personnel relations affecting both U.S. and local workers. This includes hiring local workers and arranging labor and management agreements. Management officers based in Washington, D.C., do similar work and act as liaison between the Department of State and their overseas colleagues.

Consular officers help and advise U.S. citizens abroad as well as foreigners wishing to enter the United States as visitors or residents. They provide medical, legal, personal, and travel assistance to U.S. citizens in cases of accidents or emergencies, such as helping those without money to return home, finding lost relatives, visiting and advising those in foreign jails, and distributing Social Security checks and other federal benefits to eligible people. They issue passports, register births and deaths and other information, serve as notaries public, and take testimony needed by courts in the United States. In addition, these officers issue visas to foreign nationals who want to enter the United States and decide which of them are eligible for citizenship. Consular officers located in the Bureau of Consular Affairs in Washington, D.C., provide support and help for their fellow officers abroad.

Economic and commercial affairs may be handled by one officer at a small post or divided between two full-time officers at a large post. *Economic officers* study the structure of a country's economy and the way it functions to determine how the United States might be affected by trends, trade patterns, and methods of setting prices. Their analysis of the economic data, based on a thorough understanding of the international monetary system, is passed along to their counterparts in Washington, D.C. Economic officers in Washington, D.C., write position papers for the State Department and the White House, suggesting U.S. policies to help improve economic conditions in foreign nations.

Commercial officers concern themselves with building U.S. trade overseas. They carry out marketing and promotion campaigns to encourage foreign countries to do business with the United States. When they learn of potential trade and investment opportunities abroad, they inform U.S. companies that might be interested. They then help the firms find local agents and advise them about local business practices. Most commercial officers are members of the U.S. Commercial Service of the U.S. Department of Commerce.

Political officers overseas convey the views and position of the United States to government officials of the countries where they are based. They also keep the United States informed about any political developments that may affect U.S. interests, and may negotiate agreements between the two governments. Political officers are alert to local developments and reactions to U.S. policy. They maintain close contact with foreign officials and political and labor leaders and try to predict changes in local attitudes or leadership that might affect U.S. policies. They report their observations to Washington, D.C., and interpret what is happening.

Political officers in Washington, D.C., study and evaluate the information submitted by their counterparts abroad. They keep State Department and White House officials informed of developments overseas and of the possible effects on the United States. They suggest revisions in U.S. policy and see that their fellow officers abroad carry out approved changes.

The U.S. Information Service assigns *public diplomacy officers* to serve at diplomatic missions in foreign countries. *Information officers* prepare and disseminate information designed to help other countries understand the United States and its policies. They distribute press releases and background articles and meet with members of the local press, radio, television, and film companies to give them information about the United States. *Cultural officers* engage in activities that promote an understanding and appreciation of American culture and traditions. These activities may involve educational and cultural exchanges between the countries, exhibits, lectures, performing arts events, libraries, book translations, English teaching programs, and youth groups. Cultural officers deal with universities and cultural and intellectual leaders. Many officers work on both information and cultural programs.

REQUIREMENTS

High School
Those who work for the Foreign Service will need to call upon a great deal of general knowledge about the world and its history. Take courses such as social studies, history, American government, and English literature. English composition will help you develop writing and communication skills. Any foreign language course will give you a good foundation in language study—and good foreign language skills can help in getting a job with the Foreign Service and make you eligible for a higher starting salary. Take a journalism course in which you'll be following current events and world news, as well as developing your writing and editing skills. Accounting, math, business, and economics classes will give you a good background for dealing with foreign trade issues.

Postsecondary Training
Though the Foreign Service is open to any United States citizen between the ages of 21 and 59 who passes the written, oral, and

physical examinations, you'll need at least a bachelor's degree to be competitive and to have the knowledge necessary for completing the exam. Most Foreign Service officers have graduate degrees. Regardless of the level of education, candidates are expected to have a broad knowledge of foreign and domestic affairs and to be well informed on U.S. history, government, economics, culture, literature, and business administration. The fields of study most often chosen by those with a higher education include history, international relations, political science, economics, law, English literature, and foreign languages. The Georgetown University Edmund A. Walsh School of Foreign Service (http://www.georgetown.edu/sfs) has undergraduate and graduate programs designed to prepare students for careers in international affairs. Many luminaries have graduated from the school, including Bill Clinton in 1968. Former Secretary of State Madeleine Albright served as a member of the school's faculty.

The Foreign Service has internship opportunities available to college students in their junior and senior years and to graduate students. About half of these unpaid internships are based in Washington, D.C., while the other half are at U.S. embassies and consulates overseas. As an intern, you may write reports, assist with trade negotiations, or work with budget projects. You may be involved in visa or passport work. The Foreign Service also offers a Foreign Affairs Fellowship Program (http://www.careers.state.gov/student/programs/pickering.html), which provides funding to undergraduate and graduate students preparing academically to enter the Foreign Service.

Other Requirements

As you can tell from the education and examination requirements mentioned above, you must be very intelligent and a quick learner to be a successful Foreign Service officer. You should be flexible and adaptable to new cultures and traditions. You must be interested in the histories and traditions of foreign cultures and respectful of the practices of other nations. "Perhaps most important," James Prosser advises, "is a desire to communicate directly with foreign cultures and people. Start by learning their language and speak to them in it. That wins a lot of points in any discussion."

Good people skills are important because you'll be expected to work as a member of a team and deal diplomatically with people from other countries. But you'll also be expected to work independently. You should be in good physical condition, so that you can handle the climate variations and sometimes unhealthy conditions of different countries.

EXPLORING

As a member of a foreign language club at your school, you may have the opportunity to visit other countries. If such programs don't exist, check with your guidance counselor or school librarian about discounted foreign travel packages available to student groups. Also, ask them about student exchange programs if you're interested in spending several weeks in another country. There's also the People to People Student Ambassador Program, which offers summer travel opportunities to students in grades six through 12. To learn about the expenses, destinations, and application process, visit its Web site (http://www.studentambassadors.org).

James Prosser's interest in foreign cultures started when he was very young. "Back in the 1930s," he says, "I built a crystal radio set, which enabled me to listen to distant radio stations. That led me to discover shortwave listening, and soon I was listening to foreign countries."

The American Foreign Service Association (AFSA), a professional association serving Foreign Service officers, publishes the *Foreign Service Journal* (http://www.afsa.org/fsj). The journal features articles by Foreign Service officers and academics that can give you insight into the Foreign Service. AFSA offers a discount on student subscriptions.

It may be difficult finding part-time or summer jobs that are directly related to foreign service, but check with federal, state, and local government agencies and a local university. Some schools use volunteers or part-time employees to lead tours for foreign exchange students.

EMPLOYERS

The Foreign Service isn't a single organization. Prospective officers actually apply to join one of two different agencies: either the Department of State or the Bureau of International Information Programs. The Department of State is responsible for the development and implementation of foreign policy, while the Bureau of International Information Programs explains these policies and actions to the world by engaging in public diplomacy. When hired, officers are offered an appointment to one of these agencies. There's very little moving between agencies. Foreign Service officers work in Washington, D.C., or are stationed in nearly 180 foreign countries that have U.S. embassies or consulates.

STARTING OUT

Many people apply to the Foreign Service directly after finishing graduate school, while others work in other government agencies or professions. Some serve with the Peace Corps or the military, gaining experience with foreign affairs before applying, or they work as teachers in American-sponsored schools overseas. Some work as Congressional aides or interns. James Prosser joined the Air Force with hopes of being sent overseas. "In the back of my mind, I thought this enlistment would be my best opportunity to go abroad and experience foreign cultures." However, he was stationed within the United States for his entire four years with the Air Force. Near the end of his enlistment, one of his Air Force instructors suggested the Foreign Service.

Before being offered a job with the Foreign Service, you must pass a series of tests. The written exam consists of multiple-choice questions and an essay, and tests your knowledge of history, foreign policy, geography, and other relevant subjects. The U.S. State Department offers a study guide to help applicants prepare for the exam. The number of positions available varies from year to year; typically, thousands of people apply for fewer than 500 positions. The Foreign Service has been known to cancel its annual exam because of too few job openings.

Those who pass the written exam move on to the interview and must pass a security clearance background investigation and a medical exam. But passing these tests doesn't necessarily mean employment; passing candidates are placed on a rank-order list based on their test scores. As jobs become available, offers are made to those at the top of the list.

ADVANCEMENT

New recruits are given a temporary appointment as career candidates or junior officers. This probationary period lasts no longer than five years and consists of orientation and work overseas. During this time all junior officers must learn a foreign language. The candidate's performance will be reviewed after 36 months of service, at which time a decision on tenure (once tenured, an officer can't be separated from the service without written cause) and appointment as a career Foreign Service officer will be made. If tenure is not granted, the candidate will be reviewed again approximately one year later. Those who fail to show potential as career officers are dropped from the program.

Career officers are rated by their supervisors once a year. A promotion board decides who is eligible for advancement. Promotions are based on merit. Officers who do good work can expect to advance from Class 6 through Class 1 by the time they complete their careers. A very experienced career officer may have the opportunity to serve as a member of the Senior Foreign Service, which involves directing, coordinating, and implementing U.S. foreign policy.

EARNINGS

Foreign Service officers are paid on a sliding scale. The exact figures depend on their qualifications and experience. According to the U.S. State Department's information on Foreign Service officer benefits, starting salaries for new appointees without a bachelor's degree and six or fewer years of professional experience and those appointees with a bachelor's degree and no experience were $39,691 in 2006. Applicants with a master's or law degree and no experience, a bachelor's degree and six or more years experience, or no college degree and 12 or more years of professional experience, earned $44,399. Applicants who either had a doctorate and no professional experience, a master's or law degree with six or more years experience, a bachelor's degree and 12 or more years professional experience, or who had no college degree but at least 18 years of professional experience earned $54,794 in 2006. Salaries for career officers may range from $50,000 to more than $100,000.

Benefits are usually generous, although they vary from post to post. Officers are housed free of charge or given a housing allowance. They receive a cost-of-living allowance, higher pay if they work in an area that imposes undue hardship on them, medical and retirement benefits, an education allowance for their children, and are eligible for life insurance.

Most officers overseas work regular hours. They may work more than 40 hours a week, though, because they are on call around the clock, seven days a week. Foreign Service officers receive paid vacation for anywhere from 13 to 26 days a year, depending on their length of service. They get three weeks of home leave for each year of duty overseas.

WORK ENVIRONMENT

Foreign Service officers may be assigned to work in Washington, D.C., or in any embassy or consulate in the world. They generally spend about 60 percent of their time abroad and are transferred every two to four years.

Foreign Service officers may serve tours of duty in such major world cities as London, Paris, Moscow, Tokyo, or in the less familiar locales of Iceland, Madagascar, Nepal, or the Fiji Islands. Environments range from elegant and glamorous to remote and primitive.

Most offices overseas are clean, pleasant, and well equipped. But Foreign Service officers sometimes have to travel into areas that may present health hazards. Customs may differ considerably, medical care may be substandard or nonexistent, the climate may be extreme, or other hardships may exist. In some countries there is the danger of earthquakes, typhoons, or floods; in others, the danger of political upheaval.

Although embassy hours are normally the usual office hours of the host country, other tasks of the job may involve outside activities, such as attending or hosting dinners, lectures, public functions, or other necessary social engagements.

OUTLOOK

There is heavy competition and extensive testing involved in obtaining Foreign Service positions. Nearly 265 posts abroad are staffed by Foreign Service officers and specialists.

The Foreign Service seeks candidates who can manage programs and personnel, as well as experts in transnational issues, such as science and technology; the fight against diseases, such as AIDS; efforts to save the environment; antinarcotics efforts; and trade. The U.S. Department of State also has an increasing need for candidates with training and experience in administration and management.

Those people interested in protecting diplomacy and the strength of the Foreign Service need to closely follow relevant legislation, as well as promote the importance of international affairs. "I personally believe," James Prosser says, "that retired Foreign Service officers have a duty to tell America what we are all about and how vital it is to the national interest that we continue to always have a complete and dedicated staff in the Foreign Service."

FOR MORE INFORMATION

This professional organization serving current and retired Foreign Service officers hosts an informative Web site and publishes career information.

American Foreign Service Association
2101 E Street, NW
Washington, DC 20037-2916
Tel: 800-704-2372
Email: member@afsa.org
http://www.afsa.org

The U.S. Department of State offers a wealth of information, including internship opportunities, the history of the Foreign Service, and current officers and embassies.

U.S. Department of State
2401 E Street, NW, Suite 518 H
Washington, DC 20522-0001
Tel: 202-647-4000
http://careers.state.gov

Health and Regulatory Inspectors

OVERVIEW

Health and regulatory inspectors are employed by federal, state, or local governments to enforce laws that protect public health and safety, as well as certain regulatory laws that govern, for example, labor standards, immigration, banking, and transportation. Approximately 508,000 inspectors, testers, sorters, samplers, and weighers are employed in the United States.

HISTORY

Federal, state, and local laws have been enacted to provide service and protection to citizens in many areas of daily life. An important aspect of law enforcement involves setting acceptable standards in such diverse areas as quality of transportation and food storage and then providing ways to ensure that these standards are met. Government takes responsibility for public safety on many fronts, including various industries, labor standards, immigration, and preservation of the environment. Over the years, federal, state, and local governments have developed a system of regular inspection and reporting to assure these safety standards are maintained.

Rather than wait until a law has been violated, it is more efficient to employ inspectors to continuously watch the way in which standards requirements are carried out. For example, if a law requires that food be stored at a certain temperature to prevent the growth of microorganisms, regular inspections of the place where the food is stored ensure the law is followed, which is better than waiting until disease or illness occurs. Health and regulatory inspectors enforce compliance with all health and safety laws and regulations.

Many local, state, and federal agencies oversee the various areas of inspection and regulation that are required in such a vast nation. One major employer is the U.S. Department of Health and Human Services, which was formed in 1953 as a successor to the Federal Security Agency, which had been set up in 1939 to "administer federal responsibilities in the field of health, education, and social security." In 1979, the department was organized into five main operating components, including the Public Health Service (serving the nation since 1798). It operates a myriad of health and regulatory subagencies including the Food and Drug Administration (FDA), the National Institutes of Health, the Health Resources and Services Administration, and the Centers for Disease Control and Prevention. Other employers of health and regulatory inspectors include the Environmental Protection Agency, the Bureau of U.S. Citizenship and Immigration Services (an arm of the Department of Homeland Security), the Department of the Interior, the Department of Agriculture, the Occupational Safety and Health Administration, and many others on the federal, state, and local levels.

THE JOB

Because so many areas require regulation, there are different types of specialists within the field of health and regulatory inspection who determine how compliance with laws can best be met. The following is a list of some of the major kinds of inspectors employed by the government:

Food and drug inspectors check firms that produce, store, handle, and market food, drugs, and cosmetics. Packaging must be accurately labeled to list contents, and inspectors perform spot checks to confirm this. The weight or measurement of a product must also be accurate. The inspectors use scales, thermometers, chemical testing kits, container-sampling devices, ultraviolet lights, and cameras to test various substances. They look for bacteriological or chemical contamination and assemble evidence if a product is harmful to the public health or does not meet other standards.

Food inspectors are empowered by state and federal law to inspect meat, poultry, and their by-products to verify these are safe for public consumption. In a slaughterhouse the inspection team leader is always a veterinarian who can ensure that the animals are healthy.

Proper sanitation, processing, packaging, and labeling are constantly inspected. Specialists concerned with raising animals for consumption and with processing meat and meat products include veterinary livestock inspectors, veterinary virus-serum inspectors, and veterinary meat inspectors.

Agricultural chemicals inspectors inspect establishments where agricultural service products such as fertilizers, pesticides, and livestock feed and medications are manufactured, marketed, and used. They may monitor distribution warehouses, retail outlets, processing plants, and private and industrial farms to collect samples of their products for analysis. If there is a violation, they gather information and samples for use as legal evidence.

Agricultural commodity graders ensure that retailers and consumers get reliable and safe commodities. They may specialize in cotton, dairy products, eggs and egg products, processed or fresh fruit or vegetables, or grains. For example, eggs must meet size and weight standards, dairy products must meet the standards set for butterfat content, and other products must meet standards of cleanliness and quality. The inspectors check product standards and issue official grading certificates. They also verify sanitation standards by means of regular inspection of plants and equipment.

Agricultural quarantine inspectors work to protect crops, forests, gardens, and livestock from the introduction and spread of plant pests and animal diseases. They inspect aircraft, ships, railway cars, and other transportation entering the United States for restricted or prohibited plant or animal materials. They also work to prevent the spread of agricultural disease from one state or one part of the country to another.

Agricultural-chemical registration specialists review and evaluate information on pesticides, fertilizers, and other products containing dangerous chemicals. If the manufacturers or distributors of the products have complied with government regulations, their applications for registration are approved.

Environmental health inspectors, also called *sanitarians,* work primarily for state and local governments to ensure that government standards of cleanliness and purity are met in food, water, and air. They may inspect processing plants, dairies, restaurants, hospitals, and other institutions. This involves the inspection of handling, processing, and serving of food and of the treatment and disposal of garbage, sewage, and refuse.

Finding the nature and cause of pollution means inspecting those places where pollution might occur, testing for pollutants, and collecting samples of air, water, waste, and soil for analysis. The environmental health inspector initiates action to stop pollution and is vigilant to ensure that offenses are not repeated. In urban situations the environmental health inspector may specialize in just one area such as industrial waste inspection, water-pollution control, or pesticide control.

Environmental health inspectors in state or local agricultural or health departments may specialize in milk and dairy production; water or air pollution; food or institutional sanitation; or occupational health.

The category of health and safety inspectors also includes health care facilities inspectors, building code inspectors, boiler inspectors, furniture and bedding inspectors, marine-cargo surveyors, and mortician investigators.

Health inspectors may travel to a variety of sites such as restaurants and hospitals. The health inspectors in a processing plant generally work solely at that site, and the same may be true of dairy product inspectors and sewage processing plant inspectors. The work involves making reports to the government regulatory agency for which the inspector works, as well as to the management of the institution or company being inspected.

Regulatory inspectors perform work similar to that of health inspectors because both occupations involve protecting the public by enforcing laws and regulations relating to public health and safety.

Attendance officers, also known as *truant officers,* enforce the laws pertaining to compulsory education by investigating the continued absence of pupils from public schools.

Immigration and customs inspectors enforce the laws that regulate people and goods entering and leaving the country. *Immigration inspectors* prepare reports, process applications, and maintain records of people seeking to enter the United States. They interview and inspect passports to determine whether people are legally eligible to enter and live in the country. *Passport-application examiners* review and approve applications for U.S. passports.

Customs inspectors enforce the laws that regulate imports and exports. They inspect cargo at all points of entry to and exit from the United States to determine the amount of tax that must be paid and to check that no prohibited or dangerous goods enter or leave. Merchandise for delivery to commercial importers is examined by customs import specialists, who consider, in addition to legal restrictions, the amount of duty to be levied and such things as import quotas and trademark laws. Customs inspectors also inspect the baggage of people entering or leaving the country to ensure that proper taxes have been paid and all goods have been declared. *Customs patrol officers* conduct surveillance at points of entry into the United States to prohibit smuggling, detect customs violations, and protect our country against terrorism. Customs specialists work in the United States and throughout the world, at airports, seaports, and border crossings.

Transportation inspectors verify not only that vehicles meet safety requirements but also that the personnel who operate the equipment are properly trained to meet the standards regulated by law.

The regulations of the Federal Aviation Administration are ensured by *aviation safety inspectors* who usually specialize in general aviation or commercial aircraft. They inspect maintenance, manufacturing, repair, and operations procedures and also certify pilots, flight instructors, flight examiners, repair facilities, and schools. They are responsible for the quality and safety of aircraft equipment and personnel. State and local *motor vehicle inspectors* perform similar functions to ascertain safety and trained personnel in motor transportation. They also check truck cargoes for compliance with state limitations on weight and hazardous cargoes. *Automobile testers* check the safety and emissions of cars and trucks at state-operated inspection stations. *Railroad inspectors* have the same responsibility in their field and also investigate and prepare reports on accidents. In the maritime field, *admeasurers* take physical measurements of a ship and compute its capacity to determine the type of license, safety equipment, and fees required.

Occupational safety and health inspectors enforce the regulations of the Occupational Safety and Health Administration and of state and local governments. They are also employed in the private sector, where they have similar responsibilities. Their duties include inspecting machinery, working conditions, and equipment to ensure that proper safety precautions are used that meet government standards and regulations. *Safety health inspectors* make regular visits and also respond to accident reports or complaints about a plant, factory, or other workplace by interviewing workers or management. They may suspend activity that poses a possible threat to workers. They write reports on safety standards that have been violated and describe conditions to be corrected. They may also discuss their findings with management to see that standards will be promptly met. (For more information, see the article "Occupational Safety and Health Workers.")

Mine safety and health inspectors enforce the laws and regulations that protect the health and safety of miners. They visit mines and related facilities and discuss their findings with the miners and management. They write reports describing violations and other findings and decisions and ensure that hazards and violations are corrected. Should a mine accident occur, such as an explosion or fire, the inspector may direct rescue operations and also investigate and report on conditions and causes.

Wage-hour compliance inspectors ensure that equal opportunity regulations, minimum wage and overtime laws, and conditions relating to the employment of minors are all met. They inspect personnel records and may also interview employees to verify time and payroll information. Compliance inspectors may respond to complaints or may perform regular spot checks of a variety of employers.

Alcohol, tobacco, and firearms inspectors ensure compliance with laws governing taxes, competition, trade practices, and operating procedures. They inspect wineries, breweries, and distilleries; cigar and cigarette factories; explosives and firearms dealers, manufacturers, and users; and wholesale liquor dealers and importers. These inspectors work for the Justice Department of the federal government, and their main concern is that all revenue on these various commodities is collected.

Logging-operations inspectors see that contract provisions and fire and safety laws are adhered to and that no loss of timber is caused by damage to trees left standing.

Government property inspectors prevent the waste, damage, or theft of government-owned equipment and materials handled by private contractors.

Quality control inspectors and coordinators, sometimes called *quality assurance inspectors,* check products produced for the government by private companies to see that they meet order specifications and legal requirements. They may specialize in such products as pharmaceuticals, lumber, furniture, electronics, machinery, or petroleum products.

Bank examiners investigate banking practices throughout a state to ensure that banks comply with laws established by the government to protect against mismanagement and bank failure. They schedule audits and recommend acceptance or rejection for new institutions, mergers, acquisitions, or membership in the Federal Reserve System. They also formulate plans or actions to protect the solvency of a financial institution, acting in the best interests of shareholders and depositors. (For more information, see the article "Bank Examiners.")

Revenue officers investigate and collect delinquent taxes from private citizens and businesses. They work with taxpayers to resolve tax problems, assess penalties, and implement collection plans and criminal prosecution when applicable.

Securities compliance examiners check compliance with government regulations concerning securities and real estate transactions.

Postal inspectors enforce laws and regulations that aid in the normal functioning of the U.S. Postal Service. They investigate mail fraud and theft and perform audits in the instance of suspected mismanagement. They may also work as members of task forces with other government agencies such as the Bureau of Alcohol, Tobacco, Firearms, and Explosives and the Internal Revenue Service. They carry firearms and are authorized to make arrests.

License inspectors make sure that valid licenses and permits are displayed by establishments to which they were granted and that licensing standards are maintained. These workers may inspect one class of business such as rooming houses or taverns.

Other regulatory inspectors include weights and measures inspectors, internal revenue investigators, welfare investigators, and claims investigators.

REQUIREMENTS

There is such a variety of skills involved in these inspection jobs that the qualifications and education required depend on the area of work.

High School

The minimum education required to be a health or regulatory inspector is generally a bachelor's degree. High school students should focus on general classes in speech; English, especially writing; business; computer science; and general mathematics. Those who have settled on a career path in health and regulatory inspection may focus on biology, health, chemistry, agriculture, earth science, or shop or vocational training.

Postsecondary Training

Specific degree and training qualifications vary for each position and area in which inspection is done. For federal positions, a civil service examination is generally required. Education and experience in the specific field is usually necessary.

Certification or Licensing

Certification and licensing requirements vary according to the position. Following is a sampling of these requirements.

To be a postal inspector you must pass a background check and a drug test, meet certain health requirements, possess a valid driver's license, and be a citizen of the United States between 21 and 36 years of age.

Mine safety inspectors may have to take a general aptitude test in addition to having mining experience. They also need some specific skills, such as electrical engineering qualifications for mine electrical inspectors.

No written examination is required for agricultural commodity graders and quarantine inspectors, but they need experience and education in agricultural science.

A majority of states require licensing for sanitarians or environmental health inspectors.

Other Requirements

Health and regulatory inspectors must be precision-minded, have an eye for detail, and be able to accept responsibility. They must be tenacious and patient as they follow each case from investigation to its conclusion. They also must be able to communicate well with others in order to reach a clear analysis of a situation and be able to report this information to a superior or coworker. Inspectors must be able to write effective reports that convey vast amounts of information and investigative work.

EXPLORING

If you are interested in work as a health or regulatory inspector, you may learn more by talking with people who are employed as inspectors and with your high school counselor. Employment in a specific field during summer vacations could be valuable preparation and an opportunity to determine if a general field, such as food preparation, is of interest to you. The armed forces can provide you with valuable training and preparation in such areas as transportation.

EMPLOYERS

Approximately 508,000 inspectors, testers, sorters, samplers, and weighers are employed in the United States. Employers of health and regulatory inspectors include the federal government (mainly in the Departments of Agriculture, Defense, Homeland Security, Justice, Labor, and Treasury), state and local governments, the U.S. Postal Service, and many insurance companies, hospitals, educational institutions, and manufacturing firms. Most environmental health inspectors work for state and local governments. The federal government employs the majority of inspectors in certain areas, such as food and agriculture, which come under the U.S. Public Health Service or the U.S. Department of Agriculture. Consumer safety is evenly divided between local government and the U.S. Food and Drug Administration. Regulatory inspectors work for the Federal Aviation Administration, Treasury Department, Department of Labor, and Department of Justice.

STARTING OUT

Applicants may enter the occupations by applying to take the appropriate civil service examinations. Education in specific areas may be required. Some positions require a degree or other form of training. Others need considerable on-the-job experience in the field.

The civil service commissions for state and local employment will provide information on health and regulatory inspection positions under their jurisdiction. The federal government provides information on available jobs at local offices of the employment service, at the U.S. Office of Personnel Management, and at Federal Job Information Centers. The specific agency concerned with a job area can also be contacted.

ADVANCEMENT

Advancement for health and regulatory inspectors in the federal government is based on the civil service promotion and salary structure. Advancement is automatic, usually at one-year intervals, for those people whose work is satisfactory. Additional education may also contribute to advancement to supervisory positions.

Advancements for health and regulatory inspectors in state and local government and in private industry are often similar to those offered at the federal level.

EARNINGS

According to the U.S. Department of Labor, inspectors, testers, sorters, samplers, and weighers earned median wages of $13.76 an hour in 2004 ($28,630 annually). Earnings ranged from $8.38 to $24.77 an hour ($17,440 to $51,510 annually). Occupational health and safety specialists had median earnings of $52,640 in 2004 and salaries ranged from less than $31,560 to more than $81,670.

Health and regulatory inspectors for state and local governments generally earn salaries lower than those paid by the federal government.

Health and regulatory inspectors also receive other benefits including paid vacation and sick days, health and dental insurance, pensions, and life insurance. Most inspectors enjoy the use of an official automobile and reimbursement for travel expenses.

Most federal inspectors, including employees of the FDA, are eligible to take advantage of the Federal Flexible Workplace (Flexiplace) Project, which permits employees to work at home or other approved sites for a portion of the workweek.

WORK ENVIRONMENT

Most health and regulatory inspectors should expect to travel a considerable amount of the time. They will interact with a wide variety of people from different educational and professional backgrounds. Health and regulatory inspectors sometimes work long and irregular hours. Sometimes, inspectors will experience stressful, unpleasant, and even dangerous situations. Mine inspection can be dangerous, and agricultural and food inspection may bring contact with unpleasant odors, loud noises, potentially infectious diseases, and other difficult working conditions. Agricultural commodity graders may work outside in the heat or in cool refrigeration units. They may also be required to lift heavy objects. Consumer safety inspectors may work in slaughterhouses or processing rooms or in refrigerated storage rooms. Customs inspectors must deal with irate and angry travelers as they search luggage and cargo. They also face danger when dealing with smugglers, terrorists, and other criminals. Customs patrol officers may deal with dangerous border crashers as well as exposure to extremes in temperature as they perform their duties. Postal inspectors may encounter hazardous or explosive materials that may have been shipped improperly

A team of Occupational Safety and Health Administration specialists discusses air sampling procedures at the World Trade Center site. The team is responsible for gathering air and bulk samples for asbestos, silica, lead and other heavy metals, carbon monoxide, and numerous organic and inorganic compounds, as well as noise. (Shawn Moore/OSHA News Photo)

or deliberately through the mail. Environmental health inspectors may encounter radioactive or toxic materials or substances as they strive to make all areas of the environment safe for the average citizen.

Inspectors may face adversarial situations with individuals or organizations who feel that they do not warrant an investigation, are above the law, or are being singled out for inspection.

The work of health and regulatory inspectors is important and can be rewarding. Compensation and job security are generally good, and travel and automobile expenses are reimbursed when necessary. Inspectors can be proud that the skilled performance of their duties improves life in some way or another for every member of our society.

OUTLOOK

Government workers are generally affected to a lesser degree by economic changes than are many other workers. However, public expectations and interest concerning the environment, safety concerns, and quality products may be offset by the continuing debate concerning oversized and ineffective government and the desire for fewer regulations and strictures on daily life.

The employment outlook for health and regulatory inspectors depends on the growth of the industries or businesses they work in. The U.S. Department of Labor expects the employment of inspectors, testers, sorters, samplers, and weighers to decline through 2014 because of increased automation of quality-control and testing procedures.

Employment of health and regulatory inspectors is projected to grow about as fast as the average for all occupations through 2014 as a result of the public's concern for safe and healthy workplaces.

Some employment growth may occur at local levels, especially in the regulation and compliance of water pollution and solid and hazardous waste disposal. Growth will also occur if more power and responsibilities are transferred to the states from the federal government. In private industry, job growth will occur as a result of increased enforcement of government regulations and company policy.

Most job opportunities will arise as a result of people retiring, transferring to other positions, and leaving the labor force for a variety of other reasons.

FOR MORE INFORMATION

For additional information, contact the following organizations:
Bureau of U.S. Citizenship and Immigration Services
U.S. Department of Homeland Security
http://uscis.gov

U.S. Department of Agriculture
http://www.usda.gov

U.S. Environmental Protection Agency
Email: public-access@epa.gov
http://www.epa.gov

Occupational Safety and Health Administration
U.S. Department of Labor
http://www.osha.gov

U.S. Department of Health and Human Services
http://www.hhs.gov

For information on opportunities in Canada, contact
Canadian Public Health Association
Email: info@cpha.ca
http://www.cpha.ca

Intelligence Officers

OVERVIEW

Intelligence officers are employed by the federal government to gather, analyze, and report information about the activities of domestic groups and the governments of foreign countries in order to protect the interests and security of the United States. Federal policymakers seek specific information, or strategic intelligence, on a variety of factors concerning foreign nations. These factors include political; economic; military; scientific and technical; geographic; and biographical data. The U.S. government then uses this intelligence, much of which is classified (secret), to help make decisions about its own military, economic, and political policies.

HISTORY

The concept of intelligence gathering comes from ancient times. In a military treatise titled *Ping-fa* (*The Art of War*), written in about 400 BC, the Chinese military philosopher Sun-Tzu mentions the use of secret agents and the importance of good intelligence. Knowledge of an enemy's strengths and weaknesses has always been important to a country's leaders, so intelligence systems have been used for centuries.

Intelligence gathering has played a major role in contemporary military history. Both the British and the Americans used intelligence operatives during the Revolutionary War in an attempt to gain strategic advantage. The fledgling Continental Congress sent secret agents abroad in 1775, and Benedict Arnold will always be remembered as

QUICK FACTS

School Subjects
Foreign language
Government
History

Personal Skills
Communication/ideas
Technical/scientific

Work Environment
Indoors and outdoors
Primarily one location

Minimum Education Level
Bachelor's degree

Salary Range
$31,209 to $55,260 to $114,000

Certification or Licensing
None available

Outlook
About as fast as the average

DOT
059

GOE
04.03.01

NOC
0643

O*NET-SOC
N/A

a spy who switched his allegiance from the colonists to the mother country. Some historians have suggested that World War I resulted from poor intelligence, since none of the countries involved had intended to go to war. With the rapid developments in technology that occurred in the early 20th century, especially in electronics and aeronautics, intelligence operations expanded in the decades after World War I. Operations escalated during World War II, when the U.S. Office of Strategic Services (1929–45) was in operation. The Central Intelligence Agency (CIA), established in 1947, developed out of this office. At that time, the U.S. government believed that espionage was necessary to combat the aggression of the Soviet Union. The CIA continued to expand its activities during the Cold War, when countries were, in essence, engaged in conflict using intelligence agencies rather than armies.

Some CIA incidents have caused international embarrassment, such as when a Soviet missile shot down a U.S. spy plane flying over and photographing Soviet territory in 1960. A scandal involving illegal wiretaps of thousands of Americans who had opposed the Vietnam War caused the CIA to reduce its activities in the late 1970s, although it geared up again during the administration of President Ronald Reagan. (In 2006, the administration of George W. Bush had to defend itself against charges that it directed the National Security Agency, another intelligence-gathering organization, to illegally eavesdrop on Americans suspected of being linked to terrorism.)

With the fall of Communism and the end of the Cold War, the role of the CIA and intelligence officers changed. Emphasis is now placed on analyzing the constantly changing political and geographic situations in Eastern Europe, Asia, the Middle East, and other parts of the world. Intelligence officers are in demand to provide updated information and insight into how the political and economic circumstances of the world will affect the United States.

Today, the director of central intelligence advises the president and other policymakers and coordinates the activities of the entire national intelligence community. This community includes the CIA; the Defense Intelligence Agency (DIA); military agencies; the Department of State; the Department of Energy; the National Security Agency; the Federal Bureau of Investigation (FBI); the Department of Defense; and the Department of Homeland Security.

THE JOB

The goal of every intelligence service is to produce reports consisting of evaluated information and forecasts that political leaders can use in decision making. Intelligence officers must first decide what information is needed, gather it efficiently, and then evaluate and analyze it. *Case officers* stationed overseas are assigned to gather intelligence and then relay the information to analysts who interpret the data for their reports. Analysts' reports make predictions and forecasts about what is likely to happen in a foreign country. High-level managers review the reports and pass them along to clients, who may include the president of the United States. Specialized analysts include *technical analysts,* who may gather data from satellites, and *cryptographic technicians,* who are experts at coding, decoding, and sending secret messages.

Contrary to the impression given by spy movies such as the James Bond series, most intelligence is available from public sources, although some agents specialize in deciphering secret transmissions written in code. *Intelligence* is often misused as a synonym for *espionage,* which is only one means of collecting information. Ways of gathering information can be as simple and open (overt) as reading a foreign newspaper or as complicated and secret (covert) as eavesdropping on a telephone conversation or intercepting e-mails. Sources of intelligence include foreign radio and television broadcasts, reports of diplomats and military attachés, public documents, interviews with tourists, air surveillance, and camera-loaded satellites. Aerial and space reconnaissance, electronic eavesdropping, and agent espionage are considered covert sources.

There are three categories of intelligence operations: strategic intelligence, tactical intelligence, and counterintelligence. *Strategic intelligence agents* keep track of world events, watch foreign leaders carefully, and study a foreign country's politics, economy, military status, and scientific advances. Political intelligence consists of determining which group holds power and looking at foreign policy, public opinion, and voting statistics. Economic factors include trade agreements, the gross national product, and possible famines, all of which can influence domestic and foreign policies. Military intelligence includes the types and number of weapons, troop deployment, and readiness for battle. Scientific and technological intelligence consists of noting recent discoveries and developments in electronics, nuclear physics, and chemical sciences. Geographic factors such as border disputes can affect economic and political decisions. Gathering biographical data on current government leaders and future candidates helps complete a country's political profile. Intelligence can be "hard" or "soft." "Hard" intelligence is quantifiable and verifiable—for example, military and technological information such as the number of active troops in North Korea. An example of "soft" intelligence would be attempting to predict who will be the next leader of Bolivia.

Tactical intelligence agents gather the same kind of information as described above but do so in combat areas or volatile political settings abroad, such as in a country about to undergo a military coup.

Counterintelligence agents are assigned to protect U.S. secrets, institutions, and intelligence activities from sabotage and to identify and prevent enemy operations that would be harmful to the United States, its citizens, or its allies. Such enemy plots would include worldwide terrorism, drug trafficking, and the activities of extreme right-wing groups domestically and internationally.

Gathering information may be a routine procedure of reading the local newspaper, or it may be an exciting or even dangerous job. Counterintelligence and tactical agents generally work undercover in clandestine (secret) operations. In less-developed countries, reporting is difficult because little statistical information is available. An officer might have to go into a mine, a refinery, or a wheat field to assess economic conditions. To be effective, an operative needs contacts and sources among government officials, politicians, businesspeople, newspaper reporters, importers, exporters, and ordinary citizens. Operatives often recruit foreign agents to supply intelligence about their native countries. They may also work undercover in a job or other occupation that provides a pretext for their being in a certain place or area.

The CIA and the DIA, both major employers of intelligence officers, gather political, economic, and military information about more than 150 foreign nations in order to protect national security. The director of the CIA reports directly to the president and to the National Security Council, while the head of the DIA reports to the Department of Defense. The activities of both agencies are reviewed by Congress. The Senate and the House of Representatives each have a Committee on Intelligence that reviews CIA activities and approves the annual multibillion-dollar budget. However, many actions of the CIA are covert, and the role of the U.S. government is not publicly acknowledged until many years later. Examples include the overthrow of the Iranian prime minister in 1953 and the Chilean government in 1973.

The DIA serves the military, but its officers are not military personnel. The DIA monitors foreign military affairs, weapons, and troops; tracks compliance with international arms agreements; answers questions about soldiers missing in action; and investigates the status of prisoners of war. It also keeps track of the activities of international terrorist organizations.

The Foreign Service, an arm of the State Department, employs men and women who represent the U.S. government through embassies and consulates to the governments of other nations all over the world. These Foreign Service officers keep the secretary of state informed about all aspects of the country in which they are stationed. Called "the eyes and ears" of the United States abroad, Foreign Service officers may be diplomats, consulates, or intelligence officers.

In the armed forces, communications and intelligence specialists serve as intelligence gatherers, interpreters, cryptologists, information analysts, and translators. Domestic intelligence activities usually fall under the command of the FBI or the Department of Homeland Security. In addition, the various intelligence agencies often coordinate their activities.

REQUIREMENTS

High School
If you are interested in becoming an intelligence officer, you can begin preparation in high school by taking courses in English, history, government, journalism, geography, social studies, and foreign languages. You should develop your writing and computer skills as well. Students with the highest grades have the best possibilities for finding employment as intelligence officers.

Postsecondary Training
You must earn at least a bachelor's degree to become an intelligence officer, and an advanced degree is desirable. Specialized skills are also needed for many intelligence roles. The ability to read and speak a foreign language is an asset, as is computer literacy. Intelligence officers must have excellent analytical as well as oral and written communication skills. A historian's skills are needed to analyze political, historical, cultural, and social institutions of other nations. An intelligence officer must examine the evolution of a country, analyzing how the trends and precedents of the past relate to current and future developments.

Other Requirements
Applicants must be U.S. citizens and at least 18 years old (21 years old for some positions). High moral character, patriotism, discipline, and discretion are also essential. Because many officers are stationed abroad, they need to have the ability to adapt to changing living conditions and customs.

EXPLORING

Opportunities exist for paid and unpaid internships for college undergraduates and graduates at a number of agencies based in the Washington, D.C., area that deal with foreign and defense policy and other matters of interest to intelligence officers. The FBI, for example, runs the FBI Honors Internship Program during the summer. For more information on this program, visit https://www.fbi-jobs.gov/honors.asp. In addition to the Honors Internship Program, the FBI offers several other internship opportunities. Visit https://www.fbijobs.gov/intern.asp for more information.

The CIA runs a Co-op Program in Washington, D.C., which is open to "highly motivated undergraduates studying a wide variety of fields, including engineering, computer science, mathematics, economics, physical sciences, foreign languages, area studies, business administration, accounting, international relations, finance, logistics, human resources, geography, national security studies, military and foreign affairs, political science and graphic design." Students accepted to this program are expected to spend at least three semesters or four quarters on the job prior to graduation. You must apply six to nine months before you are available to work, and you must have at least a 3.0 grade point average. The CIA also has an internship program for students from many backgrounds, including political science and geography majors. Visit http://www.cia.gov/employment/student.html for more information on these programs.

EMPLOYERS

Intelligence officers are federal employees and can work for any one of various agencies, such as the CIA, the FBI, the DIA, the military, and other organizations mentioned elsewhere in this article.

STARTING OUT

Since intelligence officers work for the federal government, candidates usually must file a basic job application called Standard Form 171, which can be obtained from a local Federal Job Information Office. (One exception is the CIA, which has its own application process.) This form needs to be submitted with an academic transcript. The applicant's qualifications are evaluated and given a numerical rating, placed on a register, and then submitted to the appropriate government office. Agencies generally seek the best students to fill intelligence positions, so high grades are essential. In addition, each intelligence agency recruits college graduates. Agencies send representatives to college campuses nationwide to interview interested students. Candidates must undergo a medical examination and a thorough security check in addition to written and oral examinations. Those accepted into an agency generally receive one to two years of on-the-job training.

ADVANCEMENT

Extensive training programs are in place for entry-level personnel, and employees are encouraged to pursue specialized studies in foreign languages, engineering, or computer technology, for example. Entry-level employees generally are assigned to gather information. With experience and training, they can qualify as analysts. Advancement may include postings requiring more responsibility and assignments in foreign countries. Generally, officers advance according to a military schedule; they are promoted and given assignments according to the needs of the government. Further advancement leads to management positions, and all agencies aggressively follow a policy of advancement from within.

EARNINGS

Intelligence officers with bachelor's degrees generally start at levels equivalent to GS-7 to GS-11, which corresponded to a salary range of $31,209 to $46,189 in 2006. Candidates with advanced degrees may start at the GS-12 level, which paid $55,260 in 2006. Those with an advanced degree in engineering or a physical science may be offered starting salaries of $62,000 or more. Experience and additional qualifications, such as knowledge of a rare foreign language, bring higher salaries. Those in top management earn from $74,000 to $114,000 a year. Officers who work abroad receive free housing, special allowances, and other benefits. Those deployed in covert or hazardous situations also receive additional compensation. Overseas operatives and military intelligence personnel are generally allowed to retire earlier than civilian intelligence officers.

WORK ENVIRONMENT

Intelligence officers may find themselves in a laboratory, at a computer station, or in a jungle. Those working in counterintelligence and covert operations often face danger on a daily basis. In addition to gathering information to protect the security of the United States, intelligence officers may be called upon to spy on the defenses of nations hostile to the United States or to prevent foreign spies from learning U.S. government secrets. They may work indoors or outdoors in a variety of climates and conditions. Many agents travel often, and travel may include everything from jet planes to small boats to traveling on foot. Most intelligence officers, however, are employed in offices in the Washington, D.C., area or other cities. Even those agents who are not working in the field generally work long and erratic hours to meet deadlines for filing reports, especially in times of crisis.

OUTLOOK

Intelligence operations are closely linked to the world political situation. In general, people with specialized skills or backgrounds in the languages and customs of certain countries will continue to be in high demand. In the past, more than half of all U.S. intelligence activities were focused on the Soviet Union. While the fall of Communism in Eastern Europe and in the former Soviet republics greatly reduced the number and intensity of intelligence operations in these countries, other parts of the world now demand more urgent attention from all agencies. For this reason, the outlook for intelligence jobs remains good, and new officers will be hired every year. The United States has become focused on terrorist activity, particularly from groups based in the Middle East, and remains concerned with the spread of nuclear, chemical, and biological weapons. As the number of countries with nuclear capabilities increases, and as economic, political, and technological changes worldwide become more frequent, strategic intelligence gathering becomes more and more important to governments all around the world. Increasingly, governments must be able to make decisions based on predictions beyond the foreseeable future. Intelligence has become one of the world's largest industries; in the United States alone, it is supported by a multibillion-dollar annual budget.

FOR MORE INFORMATION

For information on the intelligence community and scholarships, contact
   Association of Former Intelligence Officers
   6723 Whittier Avenue, Suite 303A
   McLean, VA 22101-4533

Tel: 703-790-0320
Email: afio@afio.com
http://www.afio.com

To take a career assessment quiz and for information on career paths, recruitment schedules, and student opportunities, such as internships, visit the CIA Web site.
Central Intelligence Agency (CIA)
Tel: 800-368-3886
http://www.cia.gov/employment

For information on intelligence careers, contact
Defense Intelligence Agency
http://www.dia.mil/Careers

Federal Bureau of Investigation
https://www.fbijobs.com

National Security Agency
http://www.nsa.gov

U.S. Department of Homeland Security
http://www.dhs.gov

U.S. Department of State
Tel: 202-261-8888
http://www.careers.state.gov

For intelligence-related job listings, visit
Intelligence Careers.com
http://www.IntelligenceCareers.com

Interpreters and Translators

School Subjects
English
Foreign language
Speech

Personal Skills
Communication/ideas
Helping/teaching

Work Environment
Primarily indoors
Primarily multiple locations

Minimum Education Level
Bachelor's degree

Salary Range
$25,195 to $40,000 to
$100,000

Certification or Licensing
Recommended

Outlook
Faster than the average

DOT
137

GOE
01.03.01

NOC
5125

O*NET-SOC
27-3091.00

OVERVIEW

An *interpreter* translates spoken passages of a foreign language into another specified language. The job is often designated by the language interpreted, such as Spanish or Japanese. In addition, many interpreters specialize according to subject matter. For example, *medical interpreters* have extensive knowledge of and experience in the health care field, while *court* or *judiciary interpreters* speak both a second language and the "language" of law. *Interpreters for the deaf,* also known as *sign language interpreters,* aid in the communication between people who are unable to hear and those who can.

In contrast to interpreters, *translators* focus on written materials, such as books, plays, technical or scientific papers, legal documents, laws, treaties, and decrees. A *sight translator* performs a combination of interpreting and translating by reading printed material in one language while reciting it aloud in another.

There are approximately 31,000 interpreters and translators employed in the United States.

HISTORY

Until recently, most people who spoke two languages well enough to interpret and translate did so only on the side, working full time in some other occupation. For example, many diplomats and high-level government officials employed people who were able to serve as interpreters and translators but only as needed. These employees spent the rest of their time assisting in other ways.

Interpreting and translating as full-time professions have emerged only recently, partly in response to the need for high-speed communication across the globe. The increasing use of complex diplomacy has also increased demand for full-time translating and interpreting professionals. For many years, diplomacy was practiced largely between just two nations. Rarely did conferences involve more than two languages at one time. The League of Nations, established by the Treaty of Versailles in 1919, established a new pattern of communication. Although the "language of diplomacy" was then considered to be French, diplomatic discussions were carried out in many different languages for the first time.

Since the early 1920s, multinational conferences have become commonplace. Trade and educational conferences are now held with participants of many nations in attendance. Responsible for international diplomacy after the League of Nations dissolved, the United Nations (UN) now employs many full-time interpreters and translators, providing career opportunities for qualified people. In addition, the European Union employs a large number of interpreters.

THE JOB

Although interpreters are needed for a variety of languages and different venues and circumstances, there are only two basic systems of interpretation: simultaneous and consecutive. Spurred in part by the invention and development of electronic sound equipment, simultaneous interpretation has been in use since the charter of the UN.

Simultaneous interpreters are able to convert a spoken sentence instantaneously. Some are so skilled that they are able to complete a sentence in the second language at almost the precise moment that the speaker is conversing in the original language. Such interpreters are usually familiar with the speaking habits of the speaker and can anticipate the way in which the sentence will be completed. The interpreter may also make judgments about the intent of the sentence or phrase from the speaker's gestures, facial expressions, and inflections. While working at a fast pace, the interpreter must be careful not to summarize, edit, or in any way change the meaning of what is being said.

In contrast, *consecutive interpreters* wait until the speaker has paused to convert speech into a second language. In this case, the speaker waits until the interpreter has finished before resuming the speech. Since every sentence is repeated in consecutive interpretation, this method takes longer than simultaneous interpretation.

In both systems, interpreters are placed so that they can clearly see and hear all that is taking place. In formal situations, such as those at the UN and other international conferences, interpreters are often assigned to a glass-enclosed booth. Speeches are transmitted to the booth, and interpreters, in turn, translate the speaker's words into a microphone. Each UN delegate can tune in the voice of the appropriate interpreter. Because of the difficulty of the job, these simultaneous interpreters usually work in pairs, each working 30-minute shifts.

All international *conference interpreters* are simultaneous interpreters. Many interpreters, however, work in situations other than formal diplomatic meetings. For example, interpreters are needed for negotiations of all kinds, as well as for legal, financial, medical, and business purposes. *Court or judiciary interpreters,* for example, work in courtrooms and at attorney-client meetings, depositions, and witness preparation sessions.

Other interpreters known as *guide* or *escort interpreters* serve on call, traveling with visitors from foreign countries who are touring the United States. Usually, these language specialists use consecutive interpretation. Their job is to make sure that whatever the visitors say is understood and that they also understand what is being said to them. Still other interpreters accompany groups of U.S. citizens on official tours abroad. On such assignments, they may be sent to any foreign country and might be away from the United States for long periods of time.

Interpreters also work on short-term assignments. Services may be required for only brief intervals, such as for a special conference or single interview with press representatives.

While interpreters focus on the spoken word, translators work with written language. They read and translate novels, plays, essays, nonfiction and technical works, legal documents, records and reports, speeches, and other written material. Translators generally follow a certain set of procedures in their work. They begin by reading the text, taking careful notes on what they do not understand. To translate questionable passages, they look up words and terms in specialized dictionaries and glossaries. They may also do additional reading on the subject to arrive at a better understanding. Finally, they write translated drafts in the target language.

Localization translation is a relatively new specialty. *Localization translators* adapt computer software, Web sites, and other business products for use in a different language or culture.

REQUIREMENTS
High School
If you are interested in becoming an interpreter or translator, you should take a variety of English courses, because most translating work is from a foreign language into English. The study of one or

more foreign languages is vital. If you are interested in becoming proficient in one or more of the Romance languages, such as Italian, French, or Spanish, basic courses in Latin will be valuable.

While you should devote as much time as possible to the study of at least one foreign language, other helpful courses include speech, business, cultural studies, humanities, world history, geography, and political science. In fact, any course that emphasizes the written and/or spoken word will be valuable to aspiring interpreters or translators. In addition, knowledge of a particular subject matter in which you may have interest, such as health, law, or science, will give you a professional edge if you want to specialize. Finally, courses in typing and word processing are recommended, especially if you want to pursue a career as a translator.

Postsecondary Training

Because interpreters and translators need to be proficient in grammar, have an excellent vocabulary in the chosen language, and have sound knowledge in a wide variety of subjects, employers generally require that applicants have at least a bachelor's degree. Scientific and professional interpreters are best qualified if they have graduate degrees.

In addition to language and field-specialty skills, you should take college courses that will allow you to develop effective techniques in public speaking, particularly if you're planning to pursue a career as an interpreter. Courses such as speech and debate will improve your diction and confidence as a public speaker.

Hundreds of colleges and universities in the United States offer degrees in languages. In addition, educational institutions now provide programs and degrees specialized for interpreting and translating. Georgetown University (http://www.georgetown.edu/departments/linguistics) offers both undergraduate and graduate programs in linguistics. Graduate degrees in interpretation and translation may be earned at the University of California at Santa Barbara (http://www.ucsb.edu), the University of Puerto Rico (http://www.upr.clu.edu), and the Monterey Institute of International Studies (http://www.miis.edu/languages.html). Many of these programs include both general and specialized courses, such as medical interpretation and legal translation.

Academic programs for the training of interpreters can be found in Europe as well. The University of Geneva's School of Translation and Interpretation (http://www.unige.ch/eti/en) is highly regarded among professionals in the field.

Certification or Licensing

Although interpreters and translators need not be certified to obtain jobs, employers often show preference to certified applicants. Certification in Spanish, Haitian Creole, and Navajo is also required for interpreters who are employed by federal courts. State and local courts often have their own specific certification requirements. The National Center for State Courts has more information on certification for these workers. Interpreters for the deaf who pass an examination may qualify for either comprehensive or legal certification by the Registry of Interpreters for the Deaf. The U.S. Department of State has a three-test requirement for interpreters. These include simple consecutive interpreting (escort), simultaneous interpreting (court/seminar), and conference-level interpreting (international conferences). Applicants must have several years of foreign language practice, advanced education in the language (preferably abroad), and be fluent in vocabulary for a very broad range of subjects.

Foreign language translators may be granted certification by the American Translators Association (ATA) upon successful completion of required exams. ATA certification is available for translators who translate the following languages into English: Arabic, Croatian, Danish, Dutch, French, German, Hungarian, Italian, Japanese, Polish, Portuguese, Russian, and Spanish. Certification is also available for translators who translate English into the following languages: Chinese, Croatian, Dutch, Finnish, French, German, Hungarian, Italian, Japanese, Polish, Portuguese, Russian, Spanish, and Ukrainian.

Other Requirements

Interpreters should be able to speak at least two languages fluently, without strong accents. They should be knowledgeable of not only the foreign language but also of the culture and social norms of the region or country in which it is spoken. Both interpreters and translators should read daily newspapers in the languages in which they work to keep current in both developments and usage.

Interpreters must have good hearing, a sharp mind, and a strong, clear, and pleasant voice. They must be able to be precise and quick in their translation. In addition to being flexible and versatile in their work, both interpreters and translators should have self-discipline and patience. Above all, they should have an interest in and love of language.

Finally, interpreters must be honest and trustworthy, observing any existing codes of confidentiality at all times. The ethical code of interpreters and translators is a rigid one. They must hold private proceedings in strict confidence. Ethics also demands that interpreters and translators not distort the meaning of the sentences that are spoken or written. No matter how much they may agree or disagree with the speaker or writer, interpreters and translators must be objective in their work. In addition, information they obtain in the process of interpretation or translation must never be passed along to unauthorized people or groups.

EXPLORING

If you have an opportunity to visit the United Nations, you can watch the proceedings to get some idea of the techniques and responsibilities of the job of the interpreter. Occasionally, an international conference session is televised, and the work of the interpreters can be observed. You should note, however, that interpreters who work at these conferences are in the top positions of the vocation. Not everyone may aspire to such jobs. The work of interpreters and translators is usually less public, but not necessarily less interesting.

If you have adequate skills in a foreign language, you might consider traveling in a country in which the language is spoken. If you can converse easily and without a strong accent and can interpret to others who may not understand the language well, you may have what it takes to work as an interpreter or translator.

For any international field, it is important that you familiarize yourself with other cultures. You can even arrange to regularly correspond with a pen pal in a foreign country. You may also want to join a school club that focuses on a particular language, such as the French Club or the Spanish Club. If no such clubs exist, consider forming one. Student clubs can allow you to hone your foreign language speaking and writing skills and learn about other cultures.

Finally, participating on a speech or debate team can allow you to practice your public speaking skills, increase your confidence, and polish your overall appearance by working on eye contact, gestures, facial expressions, tone, and other elements used in public speaking.

EMPLOYERS

There are approximately 31,000 interpreters and translators in the United States. Although many interpreters and translators work for government or international agencies, some are employed by private firms. Large import-export companies often have interpreters or translators on their payrolls, although these employees generally perform additional duties for the firm. International banks, companies, organizations, and associations often employ both interpreters and translators to facilitate communication. In addition, translators and interpreters work at publishing houses, schools, bilingual newspapers, radio and television stations, airlines, shipping companies, law firms, and scientific and medical operations.

While translators are employed nationwide, a large number of interpreters find work in New York and Washington, D.C. Among the largest employers of interpreters and translators are the United Nations, the World Bank, the U.S. Department of State, the Bureau of the Census, the CIA, the FBI, the Library of Congress, the Red Cross, the YMCA, and the armed forces.

Finally, many interpreters and translators work independently in private practice. These self-employed professionals must be disciplined and driven, since they must handle all aspects of the business such as scheduling work and billing clients.

STARTING OUT

Most interpreters and translators begin as part-time freelancers until they gain experience and contacts in the field. Individuals can apply for jobs directly to the hiring firm, agency, or organization. Many of these employers advertise available positions in the classified section of the newspaper or on the Internet. In addition, contact your college career services office and language department to inquire about job leads.

While many opportunities exist, top interpreting and translating jobs are hard to obtain since the competition for these higher profile positions is fierce. You may be wise to develop supplemental skills that can be attractive to employers while refining your interpreting and translating techniques. The UN, for example, employs administrative assistants who can take shorthand and transcribe notes in two or more languages. The UN also hires tour guides who speak more than one language. Such positions can be initial steps toward your future career goals.

ADVANCEMENT

Competency in language determines the speed of advancement for interpreters and translators. Job opportunities and promotions are plentiful for those who have acquired great proficiency in languages. However, interpreters and translators need to constantly work and study to keep abreast of the changing linguistic trends for a given language. The constant addition of new vocabulary for technological advances, inventions, and processes keeps languages fluid. Those who do not keep up with changes will find that their communication skills become quickly outdated.

Interpreters and translators who work for government agencies advance by clearly defined grade promotions. Those who work for other organizations can aspire to become chief interpreters or chief translators, or reviewers who check the work of others.

Although advancement in the field is generally slow, interpreters and translators will find many opportunities to succeed as freelancers. Some can even establish their own bureaus or agencies.

EARNINGS

Earnings for interpreters and translators vary, depending on experience, skills, number of languages used, and employers. In government, trainee interpreters and translators generally begin at the GS-5 rating, earning from $25,195 to $32,755 a year in 2006. Those with a college degree can start at the higher GS-7 level, earning from $31,209 to $40,569. With an advanced degree, trainees begin at the GS-9 ($38,175 to $49,632), GS-10 ($42,040 to $54,649), or GS-11 level ($46,189 to $60,049).

Interpreters who are employed by the United Nations work under a salary structure called the Common System. In 2006, UN short-term interpreters (workers employed for a duration of 60 days or less) had daily gross pay of $474.50 (Grade I) or $309 (Grade II). UN short-term translators and revisers had daily gross pay of $183.50 (Translator I), $225.70 (Translator II), $267.65 (Translator III/Reviser I), 301.20 (Translator IV/Reviser II), or 334.80 (Reviser III).

Interpreters and translators who work on a freelance basis usually charge by the word, the page, the hour, or the project. Freelance interpreters for international conferences or meetings can earn between $300 and $500 a day from the U.S. government. By the hour, freelance translators usually earn between $15 and $35; however, rates vary depending on the language and the subject matter. Japanese and Chinese interpreters and translators earn the highest median hourly rates—approximately $45 to $50 an hour—according to a 2001 salary survey by the American Translators Association. Book translators work under contract with publishers. These contracts cover the fees that are to be paid for translating work as well as royalties, advances, penalties for late payments, and other provisions.

Interpreters and translators working in a specialized field have high earning potential. According to the National Association of Judiciary Interpreters and Translators, the federal courts pay $305 per day for court interpreters. Most work as freelancers, earning annual salaries from $30,000 to $100,000 a year.

Interpreters who work for the deaf also may work on a freelance basis, earning anywhere from $12 to $40 an hour, according to the Registry of Interpreters for the Deaf. Those employed with an agency, government organization, or school system can earn up to $30,000 to start; in urban areas, $40,000 to $50,000 a year.

Depending on the employer, interpreters and translators often enjoy such benefits as health and life insurance, pension plans, and paid vacation and sick days.

WORK ENVIRONMENT

Interpreters and translators work under a wide variety of circumstances and conditions. As a result, most do not have typical nine-to-five schedules.

Conference interpreters probably have the most comfortable physical facilities in which to work. Their glass-enclosed booths are well lit and temperature controlled. Court or judiciary interpreters work in courtrooms or conference rooms, while interpreters for the deaf work at educational institutions as well as a wide variety of other locations.

Interpreters who work for escort or tour services are often required to travel for long periods of time. Their schedules are dictated by the group or person for whom they are interpreting. A freelance interpreter may work out of one city or be assigned anywhere in the world as needed.

Translators usually work in offices, although many spend considerable time in libraries and research centers. Freelance translators often work at home, using their own personal computers, the Internet, dictionaries, and other resource materials.

While both interpreting and translating require flexibility and versatility, interpreters in particular (especially those who work for international congresses or courts) may experience considerable stress and fatigue. Knowing that a great deal depends upon their absolute accuracy in interpretation can be a weighty responsibility.

OUTLOOK

Employment opportunities for interpreters and translators are expected to grow faster than the average through 2014, according to the U.S. Department of Labor. However, competition for available positions will be fierce. With the explosion of such technologies as the Internet, lightning-fast Internet connections, and videoconferencing, global communication has taken great strides. In short, the world has become smaller, so to speak, creating a demand for professionals to aid in the communication between people of different languages and cultural backgrounds.

In addition to new technological advances, demographic factors will fuel demand for translators and interpreters. Although some immigrants who come to the United States assimilate easily with respect to culture and language, many have difficulty learning English. As immigration to the United States continues to increase, interpreters and translators will be needed to help immigrants function in an English-speaking society. According to Ann Macfarlane, past president of the American Translators Association, "community interpreting" for immigrants and refugees is a challenging area requiring qualified language professionals.

Another demographic factor influencing the interpreting and translating fields is the growth in overseas travel. Americans on average are spending an increasing amount of money on travel, especially to foreign countries. The resulting growth of the travel industry will create a need for interpreters to lead tours, both at home and abroad.

In addition to leisure travel, business travel is spurring the need for more translators and interpreters. With workers traveling abroad in growing numbers to attend meetings, conferences, and seminars with overseas clients, interpreters and translators will be needed to help bridge both the language and cultural gaps.

While no more than a few thousand interpreters and translators are employed in the largest markets (the federal government and international organizations), other job options exist. The medical field, for example, will provide many jobs for language professionals, translating such products as pharmaceutical inserts, research papers, and medical reports for insurance companies. Interpreters will also be needed to provide non-English speakers with language assistance in health care settings. Opportunities exist for qualified individuals in law, trade and business, health care, tourism, recreation, and the government.

The U.S. Department of Labor predicts that employment growth will be limited for conference interpreters and literary translators.

FOR MORE INFORMATION

For information on careers in literary translation, contact
American Literary Translators Association
University of Texas-Dallas
Box 830688, Mail Station JO51
Richardson, TX 75083-0688
http://www.literarytranslators.org

For more on the translating and interpreting professions, including information on accreditation, contact
American Translators Association
225 Reinekers Lane, Suite 590
Alexandria, VA 22314-2875
Tel: 703-683-6100
Email: ata@atanet.org
http://www.atanet.org

For more information on court interpreting and certification, contact
National Association of Judiciary Interpreters and Translators
603 Stewart Street, Suite 610
Seattle, WA 98101-
Tel: 206-367-2300
Email: headquarters@najit.org
http://www.najit.org

For information on interpreter training programs for working with the deaf and certification, contact
Registry of Interpreters for the Deaf
333 Commerce Street
Alexandria, VA 22314-2801
Tel: 703-838-0030
Email: membership@rid.org
http://www.rid.org

For information on union membership for freelance interpreters and translators, contact
Translators and Interpreters Guild
962 Wayne Avenue, #500
Silver Spring, MD 20910-4432
Tel: 301-563-6450
Email: info@ttig.org
http://www.ttig.org

Judges

OVERVIEW

Judges are elected or appointed officials who preside over federal, state, county, and municipal courts. They apply the law to citizens and businesses and oversee court proceedings according to the established law. Judges also give new rulings on issues not previously decided. Approximately 47,000 judges work in all levels of the judiciary arm of the United States.

HISTORY

The tradition of governing people by laws has been established over centuries. Societies have built up systems of law that have been studied and drawn upon by later governments. The earliest known law is the Code of Hammurabi, developed about 1800 BC by the ruler of the Sumerians. Another early set of laws was the Law of Moses, known as the Ten Commandments. Much modern European law was organized and refined by legal experts assembled by Napoleon; their body of law was known as the Napoleonic Code. English colonists coming to America brought English common law, from which American laws have grown. In areas of the United States that were heavily settled by Spanish colonists, there are traces of Spanish law.

The Constitution of the United States, adopted in 1787, is the supreme law of the land. It created three branches of government—executive, legislative, and judicial—to act as checks upon one another. It also stipulated that "[t]he judicial Power of the United States, shall be vested in one supreme Court, and in such inferior Courts as the Congress from time to time ordain and establish." The Supreme Court was created by the Judiciary Act of September 24, 1789. The Supreme Court is the highest court of the

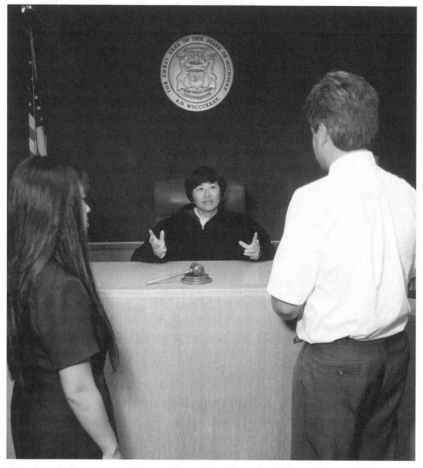

A judge discusses a ruling with a defendant (right) and his lawyer.
(Dennis Macdonald/Index Stock Imagery)

land and rules on issues related to the U.S. Constitution. The Supreme Court is made up of nine justices, appointed by the president with consent of the Senate, whose members review selected decisions made at the state level.

The Circuit Court of Appeals deals with appeals of decisions made by the district courts and reviews judgments of lower courts.

The district courts are the third level of the federal court system, servicing approximately 100 zones, or districts, across the country.

Each state also has its own judicial system, which is separate from the federal system. Most civil and criminal cases are tried in state courts. These cases can move on to federal court if they are related to an issue concerning the U.S. Constitution. Most cities also have municipal courts to handle minor cases.

THE JOB

Judges are most often lawyers who have either been elected or appointed and preside over federal, state, county, or municipal courts. Federal and state judges are usually required to have a law degree; approximately 40 states allow those with a bachelor's degree and work experience to hold limited-jurisdiction judgeships.

Judges administer court procedures during trials and hearings and establish new rules on questions where standard procedures have not previously been set. They read or listen to claims made by parties involved in civil suits and make decisions based on facts, applicable statutes, and prior court decisions. They examine evidence in criminal cases to see if it supports the charges. Judges listen to the presentation of cases, rule on the admission of evidence and testimony, and settle disputes between attorneys. They instruct juries on their duties and advise them of laws that apply to the case. They sentence defendants found guilty of criminal charges and decide who is responsible in nonjury civil cases. Besides their work in the courtroom, judges also research legal matters, study prior rulings, write opinions, and keep abreast of legislation that may affect their rulings.

Some judges have other titles such as *magistrate,* or *justice,* and preside over a limited jurisdiction. Magistrates hear civil cases in which damages do not exceed a prescribed maximum, as well as minor misdemeanor cases that do not involve penitentiary sentences or fines that exceed a certain specified amount.

REQUIREMENTS

High School

Most judges first work as lawyers before being elected or appointed to the bench. A high school diploma, a college degree, and three years of law school are minimum requirements for a law degree. A high school diploma is a first step on the ladder of education that a lawyer must climb. If you are considering a career in law, courses such as government, history, social studies, and economics provide a solid background for entering college-level courses. Speech courses are also helpful to build strong communication skills necessary for the profession. Also take advantage of any computer-related classes, as lawyers and judges often use technology to research and interpret the law, from surfing the Internet to searching legal databases.

Postsecondary Training

To enter any law school approved by the American Bar Association, you must satisfactorily complete at least three, and usually four, years of college work. Most law schools do not specify any particular courses for prelaw education. Usually, a liberal arts track is most advisable, with courses in English, history, economics, social sciences, logic, and public speaking. A college student planning on specialization in a particular area of law, however, might also take courses significantly related to that area, such as economics, agriculture, or political science. Those interested should write to several law schools to learn more about any requirements and to see if they will accept credits from the college the student is planning to attend.

Currently, 191 law schools in the United States are approved by the American Bar Association; others, many of them night schools, are approved by state authorities only. Most of the approved law schools, however, do have night sessions to accommodate part-time students. Part-time courses of study usually take four years.

Law school training consists of required courses such as legal writing and research, contracts, criminal law, constitutional law, torts, and property. The second and third years may be devoted to specialized courses of interest to the student, such as evidence, business transactions and corporations, or admiralty. The study of cases and decisions is of basic importance to the law student, who will be required to read and study thousands of these cases. A degree of juris doctor (J.D.) or bachelor of laws (LL.B.) is usually granted upon graduation. Some law students considering specialization, research, or teaching may go on for advanced study.

Most law schools require that applicants take the Law School Admission Test (LSAT), where prospective law students are tested on their critical thinking, writing, and reasoning abilities.

Certification or Licensing
Every state requires that lawyers be admitted to the bar of that state before they can practice. They require that applicants graduate from an approved law school and that they pass a written examination in the state in which they intend to practice. In a few states, graduates of law schools within the state are excused from these written examinations. After lawyers have been admitted to the bar in one state, they can practice in another state without taking a written examination if the states have reciprocity agreements; however, they will be required to meet certain state standards of good character and legal experience and pay any applicable fees.

There is no specific certification or licensing available for judges.

Other Requirements
Federal courts and agencies have their own rules regulating admission to practice. Other requirements vary among the states. For

example, the states of Vermont, New York, Washington, Virginia, California, Maine, and Wyoming allow a person who has spent several years reading law in a law office but has no college training or who has a combination of reading and law school experience to take the state bar examination. Few people now enter law practice in this manner.

A few states accept the study of law by correspondence. Some states require that newly graduated lawyers serve a period of clerkship in an established law firm before they are eligible to take the bar examination.

Almost all judges appointed or elected to any court must be lawyers and members of the bar, usually with many years of experience.

Both lawyers and judges have to be effective communicators, work well with people, and be able to find creative solutions to problems, such as complex court cases.

EXPLORING

If you think a career as a lawyer or judge might be right up your alley, there are several ways you can find out more about it before making a final decision. First, sit in on a trial or two at your local or state courthouse. Try to focus mainly on the judge and the lawyer and take note of what they do. Write down questions you have and terms or actions you don't understand. Then talk to your guidance counselor and ask for help in setting up a telephone or in-person interview with a judge or lawyer. Ask questions and get the scoop on what those careers are really all about. Also, talk to your guidance counselor or political science teacher about starting or joining a job-shadowing program. Job-shadowing programs allow you to follow a person in a certain career around for a day or two to get an idea of what goes on in a typical day. You may even be invited to help out with a few minor duties.

You can also search the Internet for general information about lawyers and judges and current court cases. Read court transcripts and summary opinions written by judges on issues of importance today. After you've done some research and talked to a lawyer or judge, if you still think you are destined for law school, try to get a part-time job in a law office. Ask your guidance counselor for help.

If you are already in law school, you might consider becoming a student member of the American Bar Association. Student members receive *Student Lawyer,* a magazine that contains useful information for aspiring lawyers. Sample articles from the magazine can be read at http://www.abanet.org/lsd/stulawyer.

EMPLOYERS

Approximately 47,000 judges are employed in the United States. Judges and magistrates work for federal, state, and local levels of government. About 40 percent of all judges work for state and local government.

STARTING OUT

The career of judge is not an entry-level position. Judges typically start out as lawyers. Only after years of experience and careful study of the law are they appointed or elected to the bench.

The first steps in entering the law profession are graduation from an approved law school and passing a state bar examination. Beginning lawyers usually work as assistants to experienced lawyers. At first they do mainly research and routine work. After a few years of successful experience, they may be ready to go out on their own. Other choices open to the beginning lawyer include joining an established law firm or entering into partnership with another lawyer.

ADVANCEMENT

Judges usually advance from lower courts to higher courts either in terms of the matters that are decided or in terms of the level—local, state, or federal.

EARNINGS

Judges earned median annual salaries of $97,260 in 2004, according to the U.S. Department of Labor. Salaries ranged from less than $27,960 to more than $144,060.

According to the Administrative Office of the U.S. Courts, federal district court judges earned an average of $162,100 in 2005. The chief justice of the United States earned $208,100, while associate justices of the Supreme Court earned $199,200 in 2005. A survey conducted by the National Center for State Courts reports that the 2004 average salaries for associate judges in the states' highest courts ranged from $95,000 to $175,575. At the state level, judges serving in intermediate appellate courts ranged from $94,212 to $164,604, and in general jurisdiction trial courts, salaries ranged from $88,164 to $158,100.

WORK ENVIRONMENT

Courtrooms are usually pleasant, although busy, places to work. Some courts, such as small claims, family, or surrogate, may have evening hours to provide flexibility to the community. Criminal arraignments may be held at any time of the day or night. Court hours for most judges are usually regular business hours, with a one-hour lunch break.

OUTLOOK

Employment of judges is expected to grow about as fast as the average through 2012. Demand for judges should grow as the public focuses more on crime, as well as to litigate disputes that were previously handled out of court. Despite this prediction, budgetary cuts may limit the hiring of new judges—especially at the federal level. Judges who retire, however, will need to be replaced. There may be an increase in judges in cities with large population growth, but competition will be high for any openings.

FOR MORE INFORMATION

For information about law student services offered by the ABA, contact
American Bar Association (ABA)
321 North Clark Street
Chicago, IL 60610-4714
Tel: 312-988-5522
Email: abasvcctr@abanet.org
http://www.abanet.org

For information on workshops and seminars, contact
Association of American Law Schools
1201 Connecticut Avenue, NW, Suite 800
Washington, DC 20036-2717
Tel: 202-296-8851
Email: aals@aals.org
http://www.aals.org

The FBA provides information for lawyers and judges involved in federal practice.
Federal Bar Association (FBA)
Student Services
2215 M Street, NW
Washington, DC 20037-1483
Tel: 202-785-1614
Email: fba@fedbar.org
http://fedbar.org

For information on educational programs for federal judges, contact
Federal Judicial Center
Thurgood Marshall Federal Judiciary Building
One Columbus Circle, NE
Washington DC 20002-8003
Tel; 202-502-4000
http://www.fjc.gov

For information on choosing a law school, law careers, salaries, and alternative law careers, contact
National Association for Law Placement
1025 Connecticut Avenue, NW, Suite 1110
Washington, DC 20036-5413
Tel: 202-835-1001
Email: info@nalp.org
http://www.nalp.org

For information on state courts, contact
National Center for State Courts
2425 Wilson Boulevard, Suite 350
Arlington, VA 22201-3326
Tel: 800-532-0204
http://www.ncsconline.org

For information on judicial education, contact
National Judicial College
University of Nevada-Reno
Judicial College Building, MS 358
Reno, NV 89557
Tel: 800-255-8343
http://www.judges.org

For information on the Supreme Court, such as recent rulings, contact
Supreme Court of the United States
http://www.supremecourtus.gov

MAIL CARRIERS

OVERVIEW

Mail carriers are employees of the United States Postal Service (USPS). They are responsible for delivering and collecting mail on the specific routes assigned to them. Residential carriers deliver the mail on foot and by vehicle to people in cities and suburbs. Because of the large distances between homes in the country, rural carriers drive their routes to reach customers. The USPS employs 335,000 mail carriers.

HISTORY

Through the ages, people have found ways to communicate with each other by transporting written messages over both great and small distances. In the sixth century BC, people carved messages on bronze tablets and had them delivered by horseback.

Eventually, letters written on paper were carried by horseback riders following a circuit of delivery routes. Along the different routes, fresh horses and new riders would be waiting so that the mail could be delivered as rapidly as possible. In America, this system was known as the Pony Express.

In 1775, Benjamin Franklin was appointed as the first U.S. Postmaster General by the Continental Congress and had under his jurisdiction some 50 colonial post offices. Franklin was able to introduce many improvements in the postal services, including faster mail delivery.

Airmail delivery on a regular route began in 1918; mail was flown daily between New York City and Washington, D.C. Today most mail between large cities is flown on freight airplanes.

Did You Know?

In 2006, the U.S. Postal Service:

- Had more than 37,000 post offices.

- Employed more than 700,000 career employees.

- Delivered 212 billion pieces of mail to more than 144 million homes each year.

- Served more than 7.5 million customers each day.

- Handled more than 44 percent of the world's card and letter mail volume.

Source: U.S. Postal Service

From the early days of the stagecoach and Pony Express to the fast-moving trains, trucks, and jets of today, employees of the USPS have always been a respected group of professionals. They now provide services to millions of people.

THE JOB

Of all postal employees, mail carriers are probably the most familiar to the general public. They can be seen almost every day delivering and collecting mail along their routes at businesses and private residences.

Most mail carriers begin their workday early in the morning, some as early as 4:00 A.M. In large cities, they report to the post office or substation in which they work, where they arrange the mail to be delivered. They do their sorting with "mail cases" or upright boxes labeled with names of streets, house numbers, or buildings. For Don Laird, a long-time mail carrier in California, casing the mail has its benefits: "After 14 years, it's still enjoyable to case mail—even though automation has cut the time in half—and share the time with other carriers. Casing mail is very repetitive. To pass the time you talk. As the years go by, your coworkers become almost a second family. This is an experience that is quickly passing in the American workplace, but somehow thrives at the post office."

Mail carriers must also prepare and place in their route cases reminders for special mail, such as registered letters or packages,

C.O.D. (collect on delivery) mail, and insured mail. These all involve special procedures such as obtaining signatures from recipients or collecting money. Carriers must also sign for any mail they take on their routes that is C.O.D. or has postage due on it.

Carriers make up relay bundles that trucks will carry and place in mail depositories along the carriers' routes for them to pick up during the day. Many mail carriers today drive "mailsters," which are small motor vehicles with space in the back for storing bundles of mail. This eliminates some of the need for trucks to drop off relay bundles. Some carriers who walk their routes use a push-type mail cart that enables them to carry a great deal of mail at one time. Others use large leather bags carried over the shoulder, which limits the loads to 35 pounds and necessitates using the relay system.

Deliveries in rural districts are usually made by motor vehicle. Carriers place mail in the mail boxes of each residence and pick up any outgoing mail that customers have placed in the boxes. Because a regular post office may be many miles away, these carriers may also sell stamps and money orders, process insured or registered mail, and accept parcel post for mailing. These carriers may cover routes of 100 miles or more in a single day. For Norm Spence, a mail carrier from New Jersey, delivering the mail is his favorite part of the job. "The best part of my job is while I'm out on the street delivering to my customers—especially the elderly ones. It's the highlight of their day when the mailman comes."

Parcel post mail carriers usually drive trucks and deliver package mail that is not handled by the carrier working a route on foot. The parcels are sorted by postal clerks and package sorters and put into sacks for delivery along a route.

Other types of carriers drive motor vehicles, delivering mail from a main post office building to substations and picking up outgoing mail from the substation to be sorted in the main post office. Many of these carriers are found in large metropolitan and city operations. Their duties often include delivering the relay mail bundles to storage boxes for the carriers.

Supervisors of both rural and city mail carriers are responsible for scheduling carriers' work hours, ensuring the efficiency of their routes, and investigating and resolving any complaints the public makes about a carrier's performance.

Substitute carriers usually have a combination of duties. They may deliver mail on foot or with a pushcart for part of the day and finish out their day by driving mail trucks and collecting mail from street letter boxes. They may also fill in on other types of route work when employees are sick or on vacation. They may assist regular carriers when the mail load is exceptionally heavy, such as during the Christmas holidays.

All USPS mail carriers must be able to answer the public's questions regarding postal regulations and service and to provide postal forms when requested. Many participate in neighborhood service programs, checking on elderly people or notifying police of any suspicious activities they encounter. Carriers spend most of their working hours outdoors.

REQUIREMENTS

High School
No specific formal education requirements exist for USPS mail carriers, but graduating from high school will make you a more appealing candidate for employment. Recommended high school courses include geography, business, mathematics, and physical education. Taking speech, English, and even a foreign language will help you to develop your communication skills—skills that you will need in dealing with your customers as well as your coworkers.

Certification or Licensing
Although certification is not required, applicants for USPS mail carrier jobs must take civil service examinations. The written examination is composed of three parts, the longest of which is a general intelligence test that includes questions on simple arithmetic, spelling, vocabulary, and reading comprehension. Applicants must also pass a test section that covers reading accuracy, in which they compare addresses arranged in pairs and indicate similarities or differences. The third test section examines the applicant's ability to follow instructions in making changes on a mailing scheme and in routing mail.

Prospective mail carriers may also need to pass a road test to demonstrate their ability to handle vehicles of the type and size that carriers are required to drive under various conditions. These applicants must have a valid driver's license at the time of their test appointment.

Other Requirements
To apply for a career with the USPS, you must be a U.S. citizen or have permanent alien residence status in the United States, meet the minimum age requirement of 18 years of age (16 years of age for those who have earned their high school diploma early), and pass the civil service exam and road test, if required. You must also take

eye and hearing tests. Because a great deal of mail is delivered on foot and carried in heavy shoulder sacks, applicants must also pass rigorous physical examinations to ensure that they are capable of withstanding the strenuous demands of the job. Although wheeled mail carts are being used increasingly in urban areas, which eliminates the need for heavy physical labor, carriers must still be able to stand for long periods and walk considerable distances. Their corrected vision should be within normal limits both for reading and for distance, because they must be able to read names and addresses accurately and are often required to drive postal vehicles.

A good memory is a definite asset for mail carriers. In addition to remembering many postal regulations and rules, they must be able to rely on memory when arranging the mail for their route for correct delivery. Desirable personal qualities include the ability to work cooperatively with others, the ability to follow instructions, and a degree of flexibility for performing more than one kind of job.

Lifting and loading heavy sacks of mail is often strenuous. Foot carriers in suburban and rural areas may have to carry up to 35 pounds of mail in a shoulder bag. Carriers must be able to adhere to all the pertinent postal regulations and be courteous when dealing with the public. Approximately once a year, carriers are evaluated by their supervisors on how well they perform their jobs.

Mail carriers are primarily on their own while delivering mail and are responsible for adhering to postal codes and regulations and meeting specific time schedules. They frequently have the opportunity to meet and talk with the people on their routes. Many have a feeling of accomplishment in filling a responsible job and serving the public. The majority of these workers are members of unions that represent postal employees.

EXPLORING

If a career as a mail carrier sounds interesting to you, explore the field by first observing the work of mail carriers. Take advantage of the weekend mail delivery and talk to your carrier for a few minutes about the job. You may even be able to arrange a tour of the local post office to see the sorting processes. Seek information from your high school guidance counselor for opportunities to learn more about this job.

Opportunities are sometimes available for older high school students to work part time in post offices and other companies during Christmas holiday rush periods without taking any examinations. However, preference is given to those who have taken the necessary examination and are listed on the eligibility lists.

Try to get a part-time job in the mail room of an office or large store to help you develop the skills needed for this type of work. Although no previous training is required for these positions, a business or academic high school program is a definite asset.

Don't forget the information provided by the USPS on the Web. Check out its Web site (http://www.usps.gov) for information about everything from the history of the Pony Express to how much mail was delivered this past Christmas.

EMPLOYERS

Although most mail carriers are employed by the USPS, many others are employed by private delivery companies such as FedEx, United Parcel Service, and DHL (which merged with Airborne Express in 2003). The Postal Service isn't limited to the United States. In fact, the USPS delivers more than 44 percent of the entire world's mail volume. Because mail is delivered everywhere, there are no geographic limitations to this job. Mail carriers work just about anywhere; however, there will be more opportunities in places with higher populations.

STARTING OUT

The only way to get a job as a mail carrier for the USPS is to apply through the civil service examinations. Contact your local post office to find out the date and time of the next test in your area. If you pass these examinations, you'll have a chance for a permanent position.

Examinations are scored numerically. If you receive a passing score, you are then listed on registers in numerical order according to score. When postmasters have a vacancy, they examine the registers for those who are eligible to fill the position and may select any of the top three available people for the job. The names of those people who were not chosen for the position remain on the register for consideration when other vacancies occur.

New carriers are taught how to "case" or arrange their mail on the job. They often learn their routes while working as substitute carriers or by working with full-time carriers. In Postal Service work, most employees must satisfactorily complete a probationary period of one year.

ADVANCEMENT

Most mail carriers—especially those in urban areas—begin as substitutes and advance to positions as regular carriers when vacancies occur. In general, the opportunities for promotion are limited. Carriers employed in city delivery service may sometimes advance to special, nonsupervisory jobs, such as carrier-technician, carrier foreman, or route examiner. In most cases, through seniority of service, carriers may anticipate assignments to preferred routes and regular periodic pay increases. Large city post offices undoubtedly have more vacancies and promotional opportunities than smaller offices.

EARNINGS

Full-time USPS mail carriers had median annual earnings of $45,880 in 2004. The middle 50 percent earned between $38,220 and $54,570. Salaries ranged from less than $32,080 to more than $54,570. Part-time carriers begin at approximately $13 an hour, with provision for periodic increases. Rural carriers receive salaries based on a combination of fixed annual compensation and an evaluation of the amount of work required to service their particular routes. They also receive a maintenance allowance if they are required to use their own automobiles. Substitute rural carriers receive a base pay for the days they work and the same mileage and automobile maintenance allowance given to regular rural carriers.

Full-time city mail carriers who work overtime hours in a single day receive time-and-a-half pay. Carriers also receive time-and-a-half overtime pay if they work more than 40 hours in one week.

Fringe benefits for USPS employees usually include 13 days of annual leave during each of the first three years of service and 20 days thereafter until 15 years of service have been completed. Those who stay on the job longer than 15 years are given 26 days annually. Carriers are also allowed 13 days of sick leave yearly. Other benefits include retirement plans, survivorship annuities, optional participation in low-cost group life and health insurance programs, and workers' compensation for injuries received on duty.

WORK ENVIRONMENT

Conditions of work for mail carriers are often strenuous. They must perform their jobs in all types of weather, either on foot carrying a heavy mail bag or pushing a mail cart or driving in all kinds of traffic and road conditions. For a few hours every day, they work in office buildings, which are usually comfortable. Even when inside, however, carriers must lift heavy bags of mail and be on their feet most of the time. "If you like working with the public and working outdoors in all types of weather, this may be a good job for you," adds Norm Spence.

Regular city mail carriers usually work an eight-hour day and a five-day week. Rural carriers work a six-day week. Most of these employees begin work very early, at 6:00 A.M. in some cities. Carriers must cover their routes within specified time limits. When mail loads are exceptionally large, workers may feel some pressure to meet time schedules. As a result, the relationship between management and workers in the Postal Service can be strained. Some workers feel overly pressured and treated unfairly.

Postal service workers are also usually responsible for paperwork and other record-keeping duties that may require time spent behind a desk.

Recent events have brought new concerns about the safety of delivered mail. Since the terrorist attacks of September 11, 2001, actual cases and threats of mailed anthrax and other harmful chemicals have been reported. As a result, the USPS faces increased pressure to ensure the safety of mail, for the benefit of mail carriers and other employees as well as the general public. According to the USPS, local and regional post offices "are doing everything they can to keep themselves and customers safe." They have educated their employees and sent educational postcards to all public addresses describing how to identify and handle a suspect piece of mail. For more information, see the USPS Web site: http://www.usps.gov.

OUTLOOK

The U.S. Department of Labor projects a decline in employment growth for all USPS workers. The U.S. Postal Service expects mail volume to decrease through 2014, primarily because of the increased competition from other delivery services, including e-mail. Along with a decrease in mail volume will be an increase in the number of addresses to which mail must be delivered. However, automation advances in mail sorting will reduce the amount of time carriers spend sorting and give them more time to handle longer routes. Another trend expected to increase productivity and slow employment growth is the wider use of more centralized mail delivery, such as cluster boxes, to cut down on the number of door-to-door deliveries.

Applicants for mail carrier positions are expected to far outnumber vacant positions for the foreseeable future. About 40,000 postal workers are hired each year to fill positions vacated due to retirements, transfers, deaths, and employees who choose to leave the Postal Service, according to the USPS. A large portion of those openings are for mail carriers. Competition for openings is expected to remain keen, however.

FOR MORE INFORMATION

To learn more about union representation, contact the following organizations:

American Postal Workers Union
1300 L Street, NW
Washington, DC 20005-4107
Tel: 202-842-4200
http://www.apwu.org

National Postal Mail Handlers Union
1101 Connecticut Avenue, NW, Suite 500
Washington, DC 20036-4325
Tel: 202-833-9095
http://www.npmhu.org

To learn more about letter carrier careers, contact

National Association of Letter Carriers, AFL-CIO
100 Indiana Avenue, NW
Washington, DC 20001-2144
Tel: 202-393-4695
Email: nalcinf@nalc.org
http://www.nalc.org

For information about eligibility and qualifying examinations for the U.S. Postal Service, consult your local post office or state employment service. For general information on postal employment, contact

U.S. Postal Service
http://www.usps.com/employment

Military Workers

QUICK FACTS

School Subjects
Computer science
Government
Mathematics

Personal Skills
Following instructions
Leadership/management

Work Environment
Indoors and outdoors
Primarily multiple locations

Minimum Education Level
High school diploma

Salary Range
$15,282 to $50,000 to
$160,380

Certification or Licensing
Required for certain
positions

Outlook
About as fast as the average

DOT
378, 632

GOE
N/A

NOC
N/A

O*NET-SOC
55-1011.00, 55-1012.00,
55-1013.00, 55-1014.00,
55-1015.00, 55-1016.00,
55-1017.00, 55-2011.00,
55-2012.00, 55-2013.00,
55-3011.00, 55-3012.00,
55-3013.00, 55-3014.00,
55-3015.00, 55-3016.00,
55-3017.00, 55-3018.00

OVERVIEW

The U.S. Armed Forces are composed of five separate military services: the Army, Navy, Air Force, Marine Corps, and Coast Guard. These branches organize, train, and equip the nation's lands, sea, and air services to support the national and international policies of the government. Together, *military workers* from these branches are responsible for the safety and protection of U.S. citizens. Those who choose to be members of the armed forces dedicate their lives to protecting their fellow Americans. Over 1.4 million people are active members of the military services.

HISTORY

The history of the U.S. military dates back to defense forces, known as militias, used by the colonial states. These militias began to develop in the first decades of the 17th century, long before the United States existed as a country. More than 100 years later, in 1775, the Continental Army was established to fight the British in the Revolutionary War. The colonists so valued the Army that its commander and most revered general, George Washington, became the first president of the United States.

The oldest continuous seagoing service in the United States, the Coast Guard, was established in 1790 to combat smuggling. In contrast, the first American Marine units were attached to the Army at the time of its creation; these units then were made an independent part of the Navy when it was officially established in 1798.

142

The Marine Corps was considered part of the Navy until 1834, when it established itself as both a land and sea defense force, thereby becoming its own military branch.

The air service grew from somewhat unusual beginnings. The Civil War marked the first use of aircraft in the U.S. military, when a balloon corps was attached to the Army of the Potomac. In 1892, a formal Balloon Corps was created as part of the Army's Signal Corps. By 1907, a separate Aeronautical Division was created within the Army. Air power proved invaluable a few years later during World War I, bringing about major changes in military strategy. As a result, the United States began to assert itself as an international military power, and accordingly, the Army Air Service was created as an independent unit in 1918, although it remained under Army direction for a time.

With the surprise attack on Pearl Harbor in 1941, America was plunged into World War II. At its height, 13 million Americans fought in the different branches of the military services. When the war ended, the United States emerged as the strongest military power in the Western world. A large part of America's military success was due to the superiority of its air forces. Recognition of the strategic importance of air power led to the creation of the now wholly independent branch of service, the U.S. Air Force, in 1947. Two years later, the various branches of military service were unified under the Department of Defense. (Today, the U.S. Coast Guard falls under the jurisdiction of the U.S. Department of Homeland Security.)

In the years following World War II, the United States and its allies devoted their considerable military resources to fighting the Cold War with the Soviet Union. Anticommunist tensions led to U.S. involvement in the Korean War during the 1950s and to participation in the Vietnam War, which ended in the mid-1970s. Antiwar sentiment grew increasingly insistent, and soon, the policies that established an American presence in foreign countries came under new demands for reevaluation. In 1973, the draft was abolished, and the U.S. military became an all-volunteer force. The armed forces began to put great energy into improving the image of military personnel and presenting the military as an appealing career option, in order to attract talented recruits.

During the 1980s, the U.S. military increased its efforts to bring about the collapse of Soviet communism and became active in the Middle East, particularly in the Persian Gulf, through which flowed much of the world's oil supply. Later in the decade, many countries under Soviet rule began to press for independence, and, in 1991, the Soviet Union finally collapsed under the weight of its political and economic crisis, effectively ending the Cold War. That same year, the United States engaged in the Persian Gulf War.

From the early 1990s until the terrorist attacks of September 11, 2001, the U.S. military took on a new role as a peacekeeping force. It participated in cooperative efforts led by organizations such as the United Nations and the North Atlantic Treaty Organization.

Reaction to the terrorist attacks of September 11, 2001, suddenly changed the role of the military from a peacekeeping force to an aggressor in the attempt to destroy the strongholds and training camps of terrorists around the world. President Bush said the war against terrorism would likely be a sustained effort over a long period of time. U.S. troops, warships, and dozens of fighter planes were deployed to south-central Asia and the Middle East, and air and ground strikes began. In addition to military action, the administration planned to use diplomatic, law enforcement, and financial strategies against those believed responsible for the attacks. In March 2003, a coalition of nations led by the United States and Great Britain invaded the nation of Iraq, whose leader, Saddam Hussein, was suspected of creating and harboring weapons of mass destruction for potential use in terrorist attacks. Although Hussein was captured in December 2003 and a democratic government was established in Iraq in June 2004, the struggle to bring peace to this nation in transition demanded a continued U.S. military presence.

THE JOB

The general structure of the military is pyramidal, with the *president* of the United States acting as the commander-in-chief of the U.S. Armed Forces. The president's responsibilities include appointing top military officers and maintaining the nation's military strength.

The *Secretary of Defense* is an appointed position usually awarded to a civilian. He or she is a member of the president's cabinet, presiding over the Department of Defense and directing the operations of all military branches except the U.S. Coast Guard (which falls under the jurisdiction of the U.S. Department of Homeland Security.). The *Joint Chiefs of Staff*—the senior commanders of the different services—work with the Secretary of Defense to advise the president on military matters.

Together under the auspices of the Department of Defense (the Army, Navy, Air Force, and Marines), and the U.S. Department of Homeland Security (Coast Guard), the individual services compose the armed forces. The Army is the senior service. It is traditionally known as the branch that fights on land. The Navy, more than any of the other services, has a special way of life. Its officers and enlisted people work and live together at sea for long periods, which is a lifestyle that demands close attention to duties and teamwork. The Air

Force, the newest of all the services, is highly technical and appeals to those interested in aviation and mechanical trades. The Marines operate on land and sea, and they usually form the advance troops in military operations. The corps is closely associated with the Navy and, like the Navy, prides itself on meeting the highest possible standards in training, military bearing, and discipline. Apart from more military duties, Marines provide security on Navy property and guard U.S. embassies and consulates around the world. The Coast Guard is the smallest of the military services and, as such, offers unique opportunities. It is responsible largely for the enforcement of maritime law but is perhaps most well known for its involvement in search and rescue efforts, aiding those in distress at sea. Although opportunities exist for overseas assignments, most duties in the Coast Guard are related to the waters and shores of the United States.

Military workers fall under two broad occupational categories: enlisted personnel and officers. *Enlisted personnel* execute the daily operations of the military and are considered noncommissioned officers. *Officers* function as managers of the military, overseeing the work of the enlisted personnel.

Both the Army and Navy maintain a third classification of skilled experts called *warrant officers*. Enlisted soldiers or civilians who demonstrate technical and tactical ability in any one of several dozen occupational specialties may qualify as a warrant officer. Warrant officers have highly specialized training and gain additional expertise by operating, maintaining, and managing the services' equipment, support activities, or technical systems throughout their careers. Specialties include missile systems, military intelligence, telecommunications, legal administration, and personnel.

Most members of the armed forces live and work at military bases located around the world. Much of the work done on a base is similar to that done in communities anywhere. There are jobs for clerks, cooks, mechanics, electronics experts, technicians, doctors, dentists, scientists, computer specialists, and others. The military branches also employ their own police forces and intelligence and communications experts. More unusual jobs are also available. For example, the Marine Corps offers a special program for applicants with musical talent to train to play in corps bands.

In general, an enlistee, or someone just entering the military, is assigned a job based on his or her education, test results on the Armed Services Vocational Aptitude Battery, the needs of the service, and the person's wishes.

The armed forces require strict discipline from all personnel. Special military laws must be followed, and military workers must wear

A petty officer measures wind speed and direction with a handheld anemometer aboard the aircraft carrier USS Dwight D. Eisenhower. (Nathaniel Moore/U.S. Navy, U.S. Dept. of Defense)

uniforms while on duty. Those who choose to work in the armed forces can expect to move many times and also live apart from their families during their careers. Life in the military is demanding, but it does have many rewards.

REQUIREMENTS

High School

Your educational preparation will depend to an extent on your career goals. At a minimum you will need a high school degree or its equivalent to join a branch of the armed forces as enlisted personnel. If you want to become an officer, however, you will also need a college education. In either case, you should take high school classes in mathematics, including advanced classes such as algebra, geometry, and science. Take computer science classes, since many positions will require you to have technical skills. History classes, government classes, and classes covering geography will also be helpful. English classes will help you develop the skills to follow directions as well as to communicate clearly and precisely. Also, consider taking a foreign language, which may expand your job opportunities. Remember to take physical education classes throughout your high school years. You will be required to pass physical and medical tests when you apply to the service, so you will need to be in good physical condition.

Postsecondary Training

Your postsecondary training will depend on your career goals. If you wish to enter the military right after high school, you will take the path of enlisted personnel. You will agree to an enlistment contract, pledging time to the service—usually eight years. Depending on the branch you join, you may spend between two and six years on active duty and the remaining portion of the eight years in reserves. You must pass medical and physical tests as well as the Armed Services Vocational Aptitude Battery exam. Basic training comes next and will last between six and 12 weeks. During this time you will have classroom study, physical training, and training in military skills and protocol. After basic training, and depending on your skills and performance, you may be assigned to a position that calls for on-the-job training or be assigned to a job that requires further technical training. This training may last from 10 weeks up to a year, depending on the assignment. Many people combine this training with courses they take when off duty to work toward an associate's or bachelor's degree. In fact, over 37 percent of enlisted personnel have at least some college-level education. A select few enlistees are chosen for officer training after completing basic training. They receive additional military training.

If you wish to attend college after high school, you have a number of options available. You may want to attend one of the four service academies: the U.S. Military Academy (for the Army), the U.S. Naval Academy (for the Navy and the Marines), the U.S. Air Force Academy (for the Air Force), or the U.S. Coast Guard Academy (for the Coast Guard). Competition to enter these schools is intense; you will need to have an excellent academic background, involvement in community activities, and show leadership qualities, among other requirements. Most applicants also need a nomination from an authorized source, which is usually a member of the U.S. Congress. You will graduate from one of these academies with a bachelor of science degree, and you are then required to spend a minimum of five years on active duty, beginning as a junior officer.

Another option is to attend a college or university that has a Reserve Officers Training Corps (ROTC) program. In an ROTC program, you take courses in military instruction in addition to your regular college course work. After graduation you may serve as an officer on active duty for a required amount of time. Some graduates are allowed to serve in the Reserves or National Guard.

A third option for college graduates is to attend Officer Candidate School or Officer Training School. Upon completion of one of these programs, graduates enter their military branch as officers and must serve for a required period of time.

It is most important to make an informed choice when deciding on which postsecondary route you wish to take. Therefore, do as much research as you can. Talk to several recruiters, and find out what jobs are available and what position you can realistically expect to be assigned to. After all, not everyone can become a member of the Blue Angels.

Certification or Licensing

The need for certification or licensing will depend on the job you have. Pharmacists in the military, for example, must hold a license, the same as civilian pharmacists. However, it is important to note that the military does not offer certification or licensing for many jobs that require these credentials in the civilian sector. If you are interested in receiving training in the military for a certain job and plan to transfer your skills to an equivalent job in the civilian sector, you will need to do a little research to determine what, if any, additional training and/or certification or licensing you will need in the civilian workforce.

Other Requirements

To join any branch of the military, you need to be a U.S. citizen or have permanent residency status (that is, hold a Green Card). To enter the Army, Navy, and Air Force, you must be between the ages of 17 and 35. Enlisted personnel that enter the Marine Corps must be no older than 29, while those entering active duty in the Coast Guard must do so before their 28th birthday. You also cannot have a criminal record. There are height and weight standards that you should

Servicemembers Opportunity Colleges Program

Since 1972, military personnel who want to earn an associate's or bachelor's degree while they serve their country have been able to take advantage of the Servicemembers Opportunity Colleges Program. Off-duty student-soldiers can take classes at approximately 1,800 affiliated colleges and universities. These schools are located at or near U.S. military installations, overseas, and on Navy ships. Visit http://www.soc.aascu.org for more information.

ask your recruiter about, since they may vary among the services. Some jobs have special requirements, such as certain vision standards, which you will also need to find out from your recruiter.

In addition to these qualifications, anyone entering the military should be prepared for a regimented lifestyle. Those who are successful are able to follow orders, work as part of a team, and adapt well to unexpected or sudden changes. You will be required to relocate, probably several times, during your military career. To advance through the ranks, you must be willing to learn new skills as well as take on a variety of assignments. Although military life can be very rigorous, many find it both challenging and highly rewarding.

EXPLORING

You will need to do a fair amount of exploring to determine what job you would like to have as well as what branch of the military suits you. Consider any family members or family friends who have served in the military a valuable resource. Ask them about their experiences, what they liked best about the military life and what they liked least. Talk to recruiters from several branches to learn about what each has to offer you. Attend events that are open to the public, such as air shows, where you may also have the opportunity to talk to those in the service, and visit the Web sites of each branch. (See the end of this article for contact information.) Think about what job you would like to have in the civilian workplace and find out the requirements for that position. Then determine if a similar job exists in the military and ask recruiters about the probability of getting such work. After all, if you want to be an aircraft mechanic but you end up working in food service, you may be very dissatisfied for a number of years. Researching before you join is one of the primary ingredients to success in this field.

EMPLOYERS

The U.S. government employs the military. Today there are 1.4 million men and women on active duty and another 1.2 million volunteers serving in the Guard and Reserve. According to the U.S. Department of Labor, about 487,000 individuals serve in the army, 350,000 in the navy, 356,000 in the air force, 185,000 in the marines, and 33,000 in the coast guard.

STARTING OUT

A military recruiter is the person to contact for those wanting to enter the armed forces. To start out in any branch, you will need to pass physical and medical tests, the Armed Services Vocational Aptitude Battery exam, and basic training. Visit the Web sites listed at the end of this article to locate a recruiting office near you.

ADVANCEMENT

Each military branch has nine enlisted grades (E-1 through E-9) and 10 officers' grades (O-1 through O-10). The higher the number is, the more advanced a person's rank is. The various branches of the military have somewhat different criteria for promoting individuals; in general, however, promotions depend on factors such as length of time served, demonstrated abilities, recommendations, and scores on written exams. Promotions become more and more competitive as people advance in rank. On average, a diligent enlisted person can expect to earn one of the middle noncommissioned or petty officer rankings (E-4 through E-6); some officers can expect to reach lieutenant colonel or commander (O-5). Outstanding individuals may be able to advance beyond these levels.

EARNINGS

The U.S. Congress sets the pay scales for the military after hearing recommendations from the president. The pay for equivalent grades is the same in all services (that is, anyone with a grade of E-4, for example, will have the same basic pay whether in the Army, Navy, Marines, Air Force, or Coast Guard). In addition to basic pay, personnel who frequently and regularly participate in combat may earn hazardous duty pay. Other special allowances include special duty pay and foreign duty pay. Earnings start relatively low but increase on a fairly regular basis as individuals advance in rank. When reviewing earnings, it is important to keep in mind that members of the military receive free housing, food, and health care—items that civilians typically pay for themselves.

According to the Defense Finance and Accounting Service, the basic monthly pay for an enlisted member just starting out at a grade of E-1 was $1,273.50 in 2006. This would make for a yearly salary of approximately $15,282. An enlisted member with an E-5 grade and more than four years' experience earned monthly basic pay of $2,124.60 or approximately $25,495 yearly. At the top grade of E-9, a person with more than 12 years' experience made $4,113.30 per month or approximately $49,360 per year.

Pay for officers is much higher than for enlistees. According to the Defense Finance and Accounting Service, officers starting out at a grade of O-1 received basic monthly pay of $2,416.20 in 2006. This would make for an annual salary of approximately $28,994. An officer with the grade O-5 and more than four years of experience earned $5,177.10 per month or approximately $62,125 per year. And an officer with the top grade of O-10 and more than 20 years of experience had monthly basic earnings of $13,365 or approximately $160,380 annually.

Additional benefits for military personnel include uniform allowances, 30 days' paid vacation time per year, and the opportunity to retire after 20 years of service. Generally, those retiring will receive 40 percent of the average of the highest three years of their base pay. This amount rises incrementally, reaching 75 percent of the average of the highest three years of base pay after 30 years of service. All retirement provisions are subject to change, however, and you should verify them as well as current salary information before you enlist. Those who retire after 20 years of service are usually in their 40s and thus have plenty of time, as well as an accumulation of skills, with which to start a second career.

WORK ENVIRONMENT

The work environment for military personnel depends a great deal on what branch of service they are in and what their specific job is. For example, someone serving on a submarine will spend months living in extremely close quarters at sea; someone else working at a military hospital will experience the hustle and bustle of a health care facility; and an individual assigned to an international peacekeeping force may work in the tense atmosphere of a fragile truce between two bitter enemies. No matter what the job, however, strict discipline and adherence to regulations are required in all branches of the military.

OUTLOOK

Career opportunities in the military services are widespread. Today each service branch is aiming to function on a "steady state." This means every year each branch needs enough recruits to replace those leaving the service. According to the U.S. Department of Labor, approximately 170,000 new enlistees and officers must join annually to fill vacated spots. In recent years some branches, such as the Navy, have fallen short of meeting their recruitment goals, and opportunities in these branches are even more plentiful than the average. While political and economic conditions will have an influence on the military's duties and employment outlook, it is a fact that the country will always need the armed forces, both for defense and to protect its interests and citizens around the world.

In the coming years, the primary barrier to obtaining a position in the services will not be a lack of available jobs but rather the increasingly high education standards that new recruits must meet. As jobs become more complex and integrated with new technologies, those with solid educational backgrounds, including at least some college training, will have the best chances for entering the services.

FOR MORE INFORMATION

To view the Military Career Guide Online, *which contains comprehensive information on opportunities in all branches of the service, visit the following Web site:*
Military Career Guide Online
http://www.militarycareers.com

To get information on specific branches of the military, check out this site, which is the home of ArmyTimes.com, NavyTimes.com, AirForceTimes.com, and MarineCorpsTimes.com:
Military City
http://www.militarycity.com

Each of the following services publishes handbooks, fact sheets, and pamphlets describing entrance requirements, training, advancement possibilities, and other aspects of military careers. For more information, contact the following offices or your local recruiter:
United States Marine Corps Recruiting Command
Tel: 800-MARINES
http://www.marines.com

United States Navy Recruiting Command
Tel: 800-USA-NAVY
http://www.navy.com

United States Air Force Recruiting Service, Headquarters
Tel: 800-423-USAF
http://www.airforce.com

United States Army Recruiting Command, Headquarters
Tel: 800-USA-ARMY
http://www.goarmy.com

United States Coast Guard Recruiting
Tel: 877-669-8724
http://www.uscg.mil/jobs

National Park Service Employees

OVERVIEW

National Park Service (NPS) employees have a wide variety of backgrounds and capabilities and fill a number of different positions. They include law enforcement rangers, interpreters, resource managers, historians, archaeologists, clerical assistants, maintenance workers, and scientists—to name just a few. No matter what their responsibilities, these employees are all dedicated to the mission of the NPS: Conserving the natural and cultural resources of America's national parks for the enjoyment, education, and inspiration of the present and future generations.

HISTORY

The National Park System was initiated by the United States Congress in 1872, during the administration of President Ulysses S. Grant, when Yellowstone National Park was created. This landmark act established Yellowstone as "a public park or pleasuring ground for the benefit and enjoyment of people."

On August 25, 1916, President Woodrow Wilson signed an act creating the National Park Service as a federal bureau within the Department of the Interior. Its mission is to preserve, protect, and manage the national, cultural, historical, and recreational areas of the National Park System. In 1916, the Park System contained fewer than 1 million acres. Today, the country's national parks cover more than 84 million acres of mountains, plains, deserts, swamps, historic sites, lakeshores, forests, rivers, battlefields, memorials, archaeological properties, and recreation areas.

THE JOB

Our country's National Park System spans the country. With only one exception (Delaware), every state and several territories are home to at least one unit of the NPS. Most of these parks and historic sites welcome hundreds of thousands of visitors each year. To keep this amazing organization running, the National Park Service employs more than 9,000 permanent employees. An additional 11,000 seasonal employees help out during peak visitation seasons. Each NPS employee performs an essential function within the system. Here are a few examples:

Maintenance workers remove litter and keep the parks clean and beautiful. They also groom hiking trails, repair potholes, and restore historic buildings. Were it not for these hardworking individuals, our parks would soon deteriorate. Our nation's precious natural resources would be trampled and millions of park visitors each year would be disappointed.

Scientists, historians, and *archaeologists* are behind-the-scenes workers within the National Park System. Scientists help us better understand the ecosystems within our parks so we can manage and use them more wisely. By studying the cultural artifacts within our parks, historians and archaeologists are able to help visitors learn about our country's past, the momentous events that shaped our nation, and the way our natural resources influenced those events.

The NPS employees who probably have the most contact with visitors are *park rangers*. Although all rangers are trained to respond to emergency situations, there are actually two distinct kinds of rangers: those who enforce the rules and protect the park resources and those who interpret the resources for the public. (For more information, see the article "Park Rangers.")

Enforcement rangers patrol the vast expanses of our national parks, helping visitors have safe, enjoyable experiences in the wilderness. They are responsible for visitor protection, resource protection, law enforcement, and overseeing special park uses, such as commercial filming. They also collect park fees, provide emergency medical services, fight fires, and conduct wilderness rescues. To perform their responsibilities, they must spend a great deal of time in the field. Fieldwork may involve hiking the park's trails, patrolling the park's waters in boats, or interacting with visitors.

Interpretive rangers are responsible for helping visitors understand the cultural and natural resources within our national parks.

They try to educate the public about the history and value of the resources. They also try to help visitors learn how to have enriching, enjoyable experiences in the parks without harming the resources.

Interpretive rangers give presentations, lead guided tours and hikes, and answer questions. Some conduct orientation sessions for visitors as they enter the park. Some also give presentations before community groups, professional associations, and schools. "Our job," explains Carol Spears, chief interpretive ranger at Channel Islands National Park in California, "is to interpret the resources for visitors. We educate people about the value of our resources so that they appreciate them and want to take care of them."

The primary duty of the U.S. Park Police is to protect lives. Police officers are hired by the National Capital Region and are initially assigned to metropolitan Washington, D.C., where most of the force operates. *Park police officers* may be assigned to areas in New York City or San Francisco, for example, and may be detailed to any part of the National Park System on a temporary basis, but men and women considering careers as park police should expect to work in a large urban area.

The *uniformed guard force* protects federal property and buildings. Guards may serve at fixed posts or patrol assigned areas to prevent and protect them from hazards of fire, theft, accident, damage, trespass, and terrorism. Most guards are located in the National Capital Region, as a subunit of the U.S. Park Police, of which they are permanent part-time employees. A few are located in other regions and some have full-time positions.

A number of positions are available in the design and construction areas. Most of the engineers, architects, landscape architects, recreational planners, and others performing related services are based in the NPS planning and design facility in Denver, Colorado. Occasionally, such positions are also available in the regional offices and parks. Positions in the biological sciences or physical sciences—geology, hydrology, or cartography—generally require advanced degrees.

Persons with backgrounds in archaeology and history (and, to a lesser degree, sociology, geography, and anthropology) conduct programs concerned with the National Park System's cultural resources. *Land acquisition professionals* and similar employees work with analysts and administrators in the Washington, D.C., office and in some parks and regional offices.

The NPS employs a limited number of museum professionals involved in exhibit design, collection management, and museum education. Most design work is conducted at Harpers Ferry Center in W.Va., where plans and designs for exhibits and visitor center exhibit rooms are created. Some *museum directors and curators* also work at Harpers Ferry, but most work in the parks, caring for their sites' collections of natural history, archaeological, historical, or ethnographic museum objects.

The employees and functions within each national park are all overseen by one individual. This person, called the *park superintendent,* is charged with making sure that our parks maintain the delicate balance between welcoming visitors and preserving natural resources. In larger parks, he or she may work with an assistant superintendent. In addition to supervising the various operations within the park, the superintendent handles land acquisitions, works with *resource managers* and *park planners* to direct development, and deals with local or national issues that may affect the future of the park.

REQUIREMENTS

High School

If you hope to join the National Park Service, you should study science and history during high school. You should also focus on developing your communication skills. Because interaction with the public is such a significant part of park careers, you may want to

10 Most Visited National Parks, 2005

Name of Park	# of Visitors
1. Great Smoky Mountains	9,192,477
2. Grand Canyon	4,401,522
3. Yosemite	3,304,144
4. Olympic	3,142,774
5. Yellowstone	2,835,651
6. Rocky Mountain	2,798,368
7. Zion	2,586,665
8. Cuyahoga Valley	2,533,827
9. Grand Teton	2,463,442
10. Acadia	2,051,484

Source: National Park Service

take psychology, education, and sociology courses. Those who plan to become rangers might also concentrate on physical education courses; physical fitness is a definite asset for people who must hike miles of backcountry trails, fight fires, and climb rocks to perform rescues.

Postsecondary Training

Although not currently required for all positions, prospective park employees should obtain a bachelor's degree. Most rangers currently in the park system are college graduates, and many believe that this will soon become a requirement. Any individual who hopes to serve as a scientist, historian, or archaeologist within the parks must have a college degree, with a major in the relevant discipline. Those who plan to become rangers should place particular emphasis on science courses.

Although there is no specific curriculum for people hoping to enter the National Park Service, you should study science, with an emphasis on environmental science. History, public speaking, and business administration courses all are useful for anyone entering this field.

Because there is so much competition for National Park Service jobs—particularly ranger jobs—many people put themselves through additional training programs to distinguish themselves from other candidates. Some, for example, undergo medical technician training programs or attend police academies. Others attend independent ranger academies to learn the fundamentals of law enforcement, emergency procedures, and fire fighting. These training programs can offer an excellent foundation for a prospective ranger.

Other Requirements

National Park Service employees need to combine two very different characteristics: They must have a keen appreciation for nature and enjoy working with the public. As Carol Spears explains, "As national park employees, we really have two missions. We must preserve the resources and we must provide for visitor use. Many times these two missions are in conflict with one another. We have to find ways to make them both happen." It can be difficult to discern what level of visitor use can be accommodated without irreparably harming the environment. Decisions regarding this have to be made by NPS management and then carried out by all employees.

Because most national park employees deal extensively with the public, they need to be friendly, confident, and able to communicate clearly. Since they usually are responsible for a wide variety of tasks, they also must be exceptionally versatile. That they work closely with nature, which can be unpredictable, means that these people must be creative problem solvers.

In addition to these general requirements, each of the positions within the National Park Service involves a set of characteristics and abilities unique to that position. Superintendents, for instance, must be good administrators and have the vision to make long-term plans for a park. Rangers must be able to react quickly and effectively in crisis situations and convey authority to individuals violating park rules. Interpreters must have extensive knowledge about the resources in their parks and should be effective educators.

EXPLORING

Hands-on experience can be a distinct advantage if you are interested in entering this competitive field. You can get this experience by getting involved in the Volunteers-in-Parks (VIP) program. Park volunteers help park employees in any number of ways, including answering phone calls, welcoming visitors, maintaining trails, building fences, painting buildings, or picking up litter. For more information, visit http://www.nps.gov/volunteer.

If you do not live near a national park, contact the Student Conservation Association (SCA), which provides volunteers to assist federal and state natural resource management agencies. The SCA brings together students from throughout the United States to serve as crew members within the national parks. These students live and work within the parks for four to five weeks at a time.

Both the VIP and SCA experiences can help you prepare for careers in the National Park Service and help you determine whether you might enjoy such careers. You can also gain valuable experience by volunteering to work in various local or state parks on weekends or during the summer.

EMPLOYERS

While the National Park Service is the only employer for people who would like to pursue this particular career, there are many, radically different national parks. People who pursue this career may work in mountainous parks such as Grand Teton in Wyoming or the Guadalupe Mountains in Texas; forested parks such as Yellowstone, which spans three western states; or marine parks such as California's Channel Islands.

The skills necessary for many positions within the National Park Service are also highly transferable. Interpretive rangers, for instance, may pursue careers as botanists, educators, or naturalists. Law enforcement rangers may consider careers as police officers, firefighters, or emergency medical personnel. The scientists who study our parks' resources may move into private research or, like the historians and archaeologists, may consider becoming educators.

STARTING OUT

Almost no one enters the National Park Service in the position they would ultimately like to hold. Individuals who hope one day to serve as a ranger or an interpreter, for instance, must begin by getting a foot in the door. Most people begin as seasonal employees, working for three to four months a year in parks that receive more visitors during either the summer or winter seasons. Seasonal experience enables people to gain an understanding of the National Park Service mission and to help determine whether they would enjoy a career in the park system.

Those who choose to continue usually try to get experience in a variety of entry-level positions or in several different parks. This process helps individuals become familiar with the complex park system. It also allows park managers to gauge their strengths and abilities. When a person has gained experience through seasonal positions, he or she may be considered for a permanent position when one becomes available. Once an individual has gained permanent employment within the park system, he or she will receive extensive on-the-job training.

If you are pursuing your first federal government position, a good starting place is the national or a regional Office of Personnel Management (OPM). Procedures for application vary from position to position. Some positions may be applied for directly to the NPS, while others require the applicant to get on an OPM List of Eligibles and/or take and pass an examination.

ADVANCEMENT

As is true of most professions, advancement within the National Park Service usually means assuming managerial and administrative responsibilities. Rangers, for instance, may become subdistrict rangers, district rangers, and then chief rangers. Chief rangers may one day become park superintendents. Superintendents, in turn, may assume regional or national responsibilities.

While this is the traditional path to advancement, no one treads it quickly. Opportunities for upward mobility within the National Park Service are limited because the turnover rates at upper levels tend to be quite low. While this may hinder an ambitious employee's advancement, it is indicative of a high level of job satisfaction.

EARNINGS

The salaries for National Park Service employees are based on their levels of responsibility and experience. Employees are assigned salary grade levels. As they gain experience, they are promoted to higher grade levels or to higher salary steps within their grade levels.

The NPS uses two categories of levels. The first, called the General Schedule (GS), applies to professional, administrative, clerical, and technical employees and is fairly standard throughout the country. Firefighters and law enforcement officers are included in the General Schedule. The other, called the Wage Grade (WG), applies to employees who perform trades, crafts, or manual labor and is based on local pay scales.

Most rangers, for instance, begin at or below the GS-5 level, which in 2006 translated to earning between $25,195 and $32,755 annually. The average ranger is generally at about the second step of the GS-7 level, which translates to a salary of $32,249. The most experienced rangers can earn $40,569, the highest salary step in the G-7 level.

To move beyond this level, most rangers must become supervisors, subdistrict rangers, district rangers, or division chiefs. At these higher levels, people can earn more than $80,000 per year. These positions are difficult to obtain, however, because the turnover rate for positions above the GS-7 level is exceptionally low.

WORK ENVIRONMENT

To say there is a wide variety of work environments within the National Park Service is an understatement. For instance, National Park Service employees might work mainly outdoors at sites such as Grand Canyon National Park, in Arizona, or Denali National Park, in Alaska; or mainly indoors at a historical site such as the Lincoln Home National Historic Site, in Springfield, Illinois; or at Independence Hall, at Independence National Historical Park, in Philadelphia. They might work at the George Washington Birthplace National Monument, in Virginia, where unique breeds of farm animals are raised; or at Isle Royale National Park in Michigan, located on the largest island in Lake Superior and noted for its wilderness area and wildlife.

Because of vast differences in work environment, people interested in working for the National Park Service should carefully consider their preferences before applying for a job with the NPS. For example, an aspiring National Park Service employee who likes working outdoors should think twice about taking a clerical or administrative job with the service. On the other hand, a desk job or some other position may be a good way to break into the field and gain experience and might eventually serve as a launching pad to other careers in the National Park Service.

OUTLOOK

Although it covers a lot of ground, the National Park Service is really a very small government agency. Because the agency is small, job opportunities are limited, and, although they are not highly lucrative, they are considered very desirable among individuals who love outdoor work and nature. Consequently, competition for National Park Service jobs is very intense. This situation is not likely to improve, since turnover rates are low and new parks are seldom created. Students interested in working for the NPS should not be discouraged, though. The National Park Service is always looking for dedicated people willing to work their way up.

FOR MORE INFORMATION

For general career information, contact the following organizations:
National Parks Conservation Association
1300 19th Street, NW, Suite 300
Washington, DC 20036-1628
Tel: 800-628-7275
Email: npca@npca.org
http://www.npca.org/flash.html

National Recreation and Park Association
22377 Belmont Ridge Road
Ashburn, VA 20148-4150
Tel: 703-858-0784
Email: info@nrpa.org
http://www.nrpa.org

For information on volunteer opportunities, contact
Student Conservation Association
PO Box 550
Charlestown, NC 03603-0550

Tel: 603-543-1700
http://www.sca-inc.org

For specific information about careers and job openings with the national parks, contact
National Park Service
U.S. Department of the Interior
1849 C Street, NW
Washington, DC 20240-0001
Tel: 202-208-6843
http://www.nps.gov

For information on federal employment, contact
USAJOBS
Office of Personnel Management
http://www.usajobs.opm.gov

═══════ INTERVIEW ───────

Diane Miller is a historian for the National Park Service (NPS). She is currently the national program manager for the NPS National Underground Railroad Network to Freedom Program (http://www. cr.nps.gov/ugrr) and has worked for the NPS since 1984. Diane discussed her career with the editors of Careers in Focus: Government.

Q. Tell us about your educational path and how these experiences brought you to a career in the National Park Service.

A. I received bachelors' degrees in history and anthropology from Ohio University in 1982 and a master's degree in history from the University of Maryland in 1984. While in graduate school, I took a summer job with the National Park Service, collecting data from National Register of Historic Places documentation for entry into a database. That led me to a permanent job working with the National Register in various capacities, mostly related to information management and records collection. Since 1999, however, I have been national program manager for the National Underground Railroad Network to Freedom (NTF) Program. In fall 2005, I returned to school at the University of Nebraska-Lincoln in the history Ph.D. program.

Q. What inspired you to become a historian?

A. I have always been interested in history, anthropology, and social sciences in general, as the study of people and cultures from another time than my own. I have found it valuable to understand history as a means of understanding our current society, politics, and culture.

Q. What are your primary and secondary job duties as a historian with the NPS?

A. The NTF program is unusual in the NPS because our role is to facilitate and encourage the work of community researchers and others interested in the Underground Railroad (UGRR). Therefore, I do not have the opportunity to conduct my own research very often. Primarily, I provide guidance and advice to others on how to document UGRR history and historic sites and help to place information on these sites within a national perspective or context. Secondarily, I evaluate documentation presented to the NPS to determine whether it is sufficient to verify UGRR associations for the historic site.

Q. What do you like least and most about your job?

A. The most frustrating part of my job is not having the resources and the time to help all of the people who request assistance and not being able to save all of the threatened UGRR-related sites. There are many things that I like the most, such as facilitating connections between people in different areas who may have similar research interests, watching the story develop as community partners follow the leads or suggestions that the NPS may provide, seeing the progress made by preserving sites and developing interpretation for the public, meeting the local people all around the country who have a passion for their heritage and keeping the stories and memories alive of their ancestors and communities, and seeing the inspiring story of the UGRR passed along to the children.

Q. What are the most important personal and professional qualities for historians?

A. Perhaps the most important qualities are curiosity. In many ways, reconstructing historical events is like being a detective. From bits and pieces of information and clues, the historian has to make sense of the past. Learning to ask meaningful questions about the past, analyze information, and objectively evaluate evidence allows the historian to develop a rich understanding of past events. The historian must be able to focus on details while keeping in mind the larger context in which the events occurred. Historians require patience and persistence for research and also creativity for devising strategies to find information.

Q. What advice would you offer students interested in this field?

A. There are many careers in history beyond teaching high school or college, both in the public and private sectors. In most cases, students should plan on graduate school—at least to the master's level—to practice in the field. There are increasing numbers of degree programs in public history and historic preservation. Practical experience such as that gained through internships, volunteer work, or part-time jobs is very valuable when considering a career in these fields. Organizations such as the National Council for Public History (http://www. preservenet.cornell.edu/employ.html) and the National Park Service's Cultural Resources Diversity Program (http://www. cr.nps.gov/crdi/internships/intrn.htm) offer paid internships.

Regional and Local Officials

OVERVIEW

Regional and local officials hold positions in the legislative, executive, and judicial branches of government at the local level. They include mayors, commissioners, and city and county council members. These officials direct regional legal services, public health departments, and police protection. They serve on housing, budget, and employment committees and develop special programs to improve communities.

HISTORY

The first U.S. colonies adopted the English *shire* form of government. This form was 1,000 years old and served as the administrative arm of both the national and local governments; a county in medieval England was overseen by a sheriff (which comes from the original term *shire reeve*) appointed by the crown and was represented by two members in Parliament.

When America's founding fathers composed the Constitution, they didn't make any specific provisions for the governing of cities and counties. This allowed state governments to define themselves; when drawing up their own constitutions, the states essentially considered county governments to be extensions of the state government.

City governments, necessary for dealing with increased industry and trade, evolved during the 19th century. Population growth and suburban development helped to strengthen local governments after World War I. County governments grew even stronger after World War II, due to counties' rising revenues and increased independence from the states.

THE JOB

There are a variety of different forms of local government across the country, but they all share similar concerns. County and city governments make sure that the local streets are free of crime as well as free of potholes. They create and improve regional parks and organize music festivals and outdoor theater events to be staged in these parks. They identify community problems and help to solve them in original ways. For example, King County in Washington State, in an effort to solve the problem of unemployment among those recently released from jail, developed a baking training program for county inmates. The inmates' new talents with danishes and bread loaves opened up good-paying job opportunities in grocery store bakeries all across the county. King County also has many youth programs, including the Paul Robeson Scholar-Athlete Award to recognize students who excel in both academics and athletics.

The Innovative Farmer Program in Huron County, Michigan, was developed to introduce new methods of farming to keep agriculture part of the county's economy. The program is studying new cover-crops, tillage systems, and herbicides. In Onondaga County, New York, the public library started a program of basic reading instruction for deaf adults. In Broward County, Florida, a program provides a homelike setting for supervised visitation and parenting training for parents who are separated from their children due to abuse or domestic violence.

The needs for consumer protection, water quality, and affordable housing increase every year. Regional or local officials are elected to deal with issues such as public health, legal services, housing, and budget and fiscal management. They attend meetings and serve on committees. They know about the industry and agriculture of the area as well as the specific problems facing constituents, and they offer educated solutions, vote on laws, and generally represent the people in their districts.

There are two forms of county government: the *commissioner/ administrator form,* in which the county board of commissioners appoints an administrator who serves the board, and the *council/ executive form,* in which a county executive is the chief administrative officer of the district and has the power to veto ordinances enacted by the county board. A county government may include a *chief executive,* who directs regional services; *council members,* who are the county legislators; a *county clerk*, who keeps records of property titles, licenses, etc.; and a *county treasurer*, who is in charge of the receipt and disbursement of money.

A county government doesn't tax its citizens, so its money comes from state aid, fees, and grants. A city government funds its projects and programs with money from sales and other local taxes, block grants, and state aid. Directing these funds and services are elected executives. *Mayors* serve as the heads of city governments who are elected by the general populace. Their specific functions vary depending on the structure of their government. In mayor-council governments, both the mayor and the city council are popularly elected. The council is responsible for formulating city ordinances, but the mayor exercises control over the actions of the council. In such governments, the mayor usually plays a dual role, serving not only as chief executive officer but also as an agent of the city government responsible for such functions as maintaining public order, security, and health. In a commission government, the people elect a number of *commissioners*, each of whom serves as head of a city department. The presiding commissioner is usually the mayor. The final type of municipal government is the council/manager form. Here, the council members are elected by the people, and one of their functions is to hire a *city manager* to administer the city departments. A mayor is elected by the council to chair the council and officiate at important municipal functions.

REQUIREMENTS

High School
Courses in government, civics, and history will give you an understanding of the structure of government. English courses are important because you will need good writing skills to communicate with constituents and other government officials. Math and accounting will help you develop analytical skills for examining statistics and demographics. Journalism classes will develop research and interview skills for identifying problems and developing programs.

Postsecondary Training
To serve on a local government, your experience and understanding of the city or county are generally more important than your educational background. Some mayors and council members are elected to their positions because they've lived in the region for a long time and have had experience with local industry and other concerns. For example, someone with years of farming experience may be the best

candidate to serve a small agricultural community. Voters in local elections may be more impressed by a candidate's previous occupations and roles in the community than they are by a candidate's postsecondary degrees.

That said, most regional and local officials still hold an undergraduate degree, and many hold a graduate degree. Popular areas of study include public administration, law, economics, political science, history, and English. Regardless of your major as an undergraduate, you are likely to be required to take classes in English literature, statistics, foreign language, western civilization, and economics.

Other Requirements

To be successful in this field, you must deeply understand the city and region you serve. You need to be knowledgeable about the local industry, private businesses, and social problems. You should also have lived for some time in the region in which you hope to hold office.

You also need good people skills to be capable of listening to the concerns of constituents and other officials and exchanging ideas with them. Other useful qualities are problem-solving skills and creativity to develop innovative programs.

EXPLORING

Depending on the size of your city or county, you can probably become involved with your local government at a young age. Your council members and other government officials should be more accessible to you than state and federal officials, so take advantage of that. Visit the county court house and volunteer in whatever capacity you can with county-organized programs, such as tutoring in a literacy program or leading children's reading groups at the public library. Become involved with local elections.

Many candidates for local and state offices welcome young people to assist with campaigns. As a volunteer, you may make calls, post signs, and get to see a candidate at work. You will also have the opportunity to meet others who have an interest in government, and the experience will help you to gain a more prominent role in later campaigns.

Another way to learn about government is to become involved in an issue that interests you. Maybe there's an old building in your neighborhood you'd like to save from destruction, or maybe you have some ideas for youth programs or programs for senior citizens.

Research what's being done about your concerns and come up with solutions to offer to local officials.

EMPLOYERS

Every city in the United States requires the services of local officials. In some cases, the services of a small town or suburb may be overseen by the government of a larger city or by the county government. According to the National Association of Counties, 48 states have operational county governments—a total of more than 3,000 counties. (Connecticut and Rhode Island are the only two states without counties.) Counties range in size from the 67 residents in Loving County in Texas to the more than 9.5 million residents of Los Angeles County in California. There are also 33 governments that are consolidations of city and county governments; New York, Denver, and San Francisco are among them.

STARTING OUT

There is no direct career path for gaining public office. The way you pursue a local office will be greatly affected by the size and population of the region in which you live. When running for mayor or council of a small town, you may have no competition at all. On the other hand, to become mayor of a large city, you need extensive experience in the city's politics. If you're interested in pursuing a local position, research the backgrounds of your city mayor, county commissioner, and council members to get an idea of how they approached their political careers.

Some officials stumble into government offices after some success with political activism on the grassroots level. Others have had success in other areas, such as agriculture, business, and law enforcement, and use their particular understanding of an area to help improve the community. Many local politicians started their careers by assisting in someone else's campaign or advocating for an issue.

ADVANCEMENT

Some successful local and regional officials maintain their positions for many years. Others hold local office for only one or two terms and then return full-time to their businesses and other careers. You might also choose to use a local position as a stepping stone to a position of greater power within the region or to a state office. Many mayors of the largest cities run for governor or state legislature and may eventually move into federal office.

EARNINGS

In general, salaries for government officials tend to be lower than what the official could make working in the private sector. In many local offices, officials volunteer their time, work only part time, or are given a nominal salary. According to a salary survey published in 2003 by the International City/County Management Association, the chief elected official of a city makes an average salary of $18,836 a year. The average salary for city managers was $92,472. Local government clerks average about $48,164, and treasurers earn $51,597. According to a survey by the association, chief administrative officers of cities and counties earned salaries that ranged from $50,000 to $265,151 in 2005.

The U.S. Department of Labor reports that legislators employed at all levels of government had median annual earnings of $18,500 in 2004. Salaries generally ranged from less than $11,920 to $72,780 or more, although some officials earn nothing at all.

A job with a local or regional government may or may not provide benefits. Some positions may include accounts for official travel and other expenses.

WORK ENVIRONMENT

Most government officials work in a typical office setting. Some may work a regular 40-hour week, while others work long hours and weekends. Though some positions may only be considered parttime, they may take up nearly as many hours as full-time work. Officials have the opportunity to meet with the people of the region, but they also devote a lot of time to clerical duties. If serving a large community, they may have assistants to help with phones, filing, and preparing documents.

Because officials must be appointed or elected in order to keep their jobs, determining long-range career plans can be difficult. There may be extended periods of unemployment, where living off of savings or other jobs may be necessary. Because of the low pay of some positions, officials may have to work another job even while they serve in office. This can result in little personal time and the need to juggle many different responsibilities at once.

New York City Mayor Michael Bloomberg greets a constituent at the 34th Street subway station. *(Ed Reed/New York City Office of the Mayor)*

OUTLOOK

Though the form and structure of state and federal government are not likely to change, the form of your local and county government can be altered by popular vote. Every election, voters somewhere in the country are deciding whether to keep their current forms of government or to introduce new forms. But these changes don't greatly affect the number of officials needed to run your local government. The chances of holding office will be greater in a smaller community. The races for part-time and nonpaying offices will also be less competitive.

The issues facing a community will have the most effect on the jobs of local officials. In a city with older neighborhoods, officials deal with historic preservation, improvements in utilities, and water quality. In a growing city of many suburbs, officials have to make decisions regarding development, roads, and expanded routes for public transportation.

The federal government has made efforts to shift costs to the states. If this continues, states may offer less aid to counties. A county government's funds are also affected by changes in property taxes.

The U.S. Department of Labor predicts that employment in state and local government will grow more slowly than the average for all industries through 2014.

FOR MORE INFORMATION

For information about the forms of city and county govern-ments around the country and to learn about programs spon-sored by local and regional governments, contact the following organizations:

International City/County Management Association
777 North Capitol Street, NE, Suite 500
Washington, DC 20002-4290
Tel: 202-289-4262
http://www.icma.org

National Association of Counties
440 First Street, NW, Suite 800
Washington, DC 20001-2043
Tel: 202-393-6226
http://www.naco.org

━━━━━ INTERVIEW ━━━━━

Mark Begich is the mayor of Anchorage, Alaska. He discussed his career with the editors of Careers in Focus: Government.

Q. What made you want to enter public service?

A. The desire to give back to my community and have an impact on the future of our community. I have been a successful business-man for more than 20 years in Anchorage and believe citizens have an obligation to serve their communities. That's why I got myself elected to the Anchorage Assembly at age 26 and why I later ran for mayor.

Q. What are your primary and secondary job duties as mayor?

A. Anchorage has a strong mayor form of government, which means the mayor is essentially the city's chief executive offi-cer. I manage a team of executives who help me oversee Alaska's largest city of about 275,000 residents and more than 2,500 employees. I am responsible for setting overall policies, developing a vision for the city, and conveying that to our residents.

Q. What are the main challenges faced by Anchorage?

A. Like many communities, [there are] not enough resources to meet community needs. When I became mayor in the summer of 2003, we faced the worst fiscal crisis in a generation—a $33 million budget gap. We fixed that, but budget pressures continue to be a problem. While Anchorage's crime rates are much better than many cities, we've embarked on an aggressive effort to add 93 officers to our police force. Finally, we work daily to encourage a pro-business atmosphere, which encourages business development.

Q. What are the most important personal and professional qualities for elected officials?

A. Honesty, openness, listening and speaking skills, innovation, and a sense of optimism.

Q. What advice would you offer to students who are interested in careers in public service?

A. Participate because you want to give back to your community, not because you want to be in a position of power. Listen to what people have to say. Never be afraid to tell people you disagree with them. Always know who you are and what you stand for.

Secret Service Special Agents

OVERVIEW

Secret Service special agents are employed by the U.S. Secret Service, part of the Department of Homeland Security. Secret Service agents work to protect the president and other leaders of the United States, as well as heads of foreign states or governments when they are visiting the United States. Special agents also investigate financial crimes. The U.S. Secret Service employs approximately 6,400 people, about 3,200 of whom are agents.

HISTORY

The Secret Service was established in 1865 to suppress the counterfeiting of U.S. currency. After the assassination of President William McKinley in 1901, the Secret Service was directed by Congress to protect the president of the United States. Today it is the Secret Service's responsibility to protect the following people: the president and vice president (also president-elect and vice president-elect) and their immediate families; former presidents and their spouses for 10 years after the president leaves office (spouses lose protection if they remarry; all former presidents up to and including President Clinton receive lifetime protection, as this law changed in 1997); children of former presidents until they are 16 years old; visiting heads of foreign states or governments and their spouses traveling with them; official representatives of the United States who are performing special missions abroad; major presidential and vice-presidential candidates and, within 120 days of the general presidential election, their spouses; and others as directed by the president.

THE JOB

Secret Service special agents are charged with two missions: protecting U.S. leaders or visiting foreign heads of state, and investigating, according to its Web site, "violations of laws relating to counterfeiting of obligations and securities of the United States; financial crimes that include, but are not limited to, access device fraud, financial institution fraud, identity theft, computer fraud; and computer-based attacks on our nation's financial, banking, and telecommunications infrastructure." Special agents are empowered to carry and use firearms, execute warrants, and make arrests.

When assigned to a permanent protection duty, Secret Service special agents offer protection wherever the protectee lives and works. For example, if they are assigned to protect the president, they protect the president while he is at the White House in Washington, D.C., as well as wherever he travels domestically and abroad. Agents are responsible for planning and executing protective operations for their protectees at all times. Agents can also be assigned to a temporary protective duty to provide protection for candidates or visiting foreign dignitaries. In either case, an advance team of special agents surveys each site that the protectee will visit. Based on its survey, the team determines how much manpower and what types of equipment are needed to provide protection. They identify hospitals and evacuation routes and work closely with local police, fire, and rescue units to develop the protection plan and determine emergency routes and procedures, should the need arise. Then a command post is set up with secure communications to act as the communication center for protective activities. The post monitors emergencies and keeps participants in contact with each other.

Before the protectees arrive, the *lead advance agent* coordinates all law enforcement representatives participating in the visit. The assistance of military, federal, state, county, and local law enforcement organizations is a vital part of the entire security operation. Personnel are told where they will be posted and are alerted to specific problems associated with the visit. Intelligence information is discussed and emergency measures are outlined. Just prior to the arrival of the protectee, checkpoints are established and access to the secure area is limited. After the visit, special agents analyze every step of the protective operation, record unusual incidents, and suggest improvements for future operations.

When assigned to an investigative duty, special agents investigate threats against Secret Service protectees. They also work to detect and arrest people committing any offense relating to coins, currency, stamps, government bonds, checks, credit card fraud, computer fraud, false identification crimes, and other obligations or securities of the United States. Special agents also investigate violations of the Federal Deposit Insurance Act, the Federal Land Bank Act, and the Government Losses in Shipment Act. Special agents assigned to an investigative duty usually work in one of the Secret Service's more than 100 domestic and foreign offices. Agents assigned to investigative duties in a field office are often called out to serve on a temporary protective operation.

Special agents assigned to investigate financial crimes may also be assigned to one of a number of Secret Service divisions in Washington, D.C., or they may receive help from these divisions while conducting an investigation from a field office. Among these divisions are the Criminal Investigative Division, the Investigative Support Division, and the Forensic Services Division. The Criminal Investigative Division constantly reviews the latest reprographic and lithographic technologies to keep a step ahead of counterfeiters and aids special agents in their investigation of electronic crimes involving credit cards, computers, and cellular and regular telephones. The Investigative Support Division offers investigative support to special agents as they conduct investigations. The Forensic Services Division coordinates forensic science activities within the Secret Service. The division analyzes evidence such as documents, fingerprints, photographs, and video and audio recordings.

The Secret Service employs a number of specialists such as electronics engineers, communications technicians, research psychologists, computer experts, armorers, intelligence analysts, polygraph examiners, forensic experts, security specialists, and more.

For more than 15 years, Norm Jarvis worked as a special agent for the Secret Service. He protected a variety of U.S. political leaders, including President Bill Clinton and former presidents Nixon, Carter, and Ford. He also protected foreign dignitaries, including the president of Sudan and the prime minister of Israel. In addition, Jarvis investigated criminal activity in a number of cities and served in the Secret Service's Montana and Utah offices.

While his primary responsibility was to investigate crimes, Jarvis was called out regularly to protect a political or foreign leader. During those times, he served as a member of a team of special agents who worked to ensure there was always a "protective bubble," a

Secret Service Special Agents protect the vice president as he travels to the inauguration of the president. *(U.S. Secret Service)*

360-degree virtual boundary of safety, surrounding the protectee, regardless of whether he or she was moving or stationary. Protective operations can be complicated, with special agents working together around the clock, using intelligence and special technologies and working in conjunction with local authorities to make sure the protectee is safe. "We don't believe anybody can do bodyguard work just by walking around with somebody," Jarvis says. "Scowls and large muscles don't mean a lot if somebody is bound and determined to kill you." While special agents don't change their protective techniques when they work overseas, they work closely with foreign security agencies.

When agents are not on a protective assignment, they spend their time investigating financial crimes. They usually work for a specialized squad in a field office, handling specific investigations involving counterfeit currency, forgery, and other financial crimes. Special agents may receive case referrals from the Secret Service headquarters, from other law enforcement agencies, or through their own investigations. Investigating counterfeit money may require extensive undercover operations and surveillance. Special agents usually work with the U.S. Attorney's Office and local law enforcement for counterfeit cases. Through their work, special agents detect and seize millions of dollars of counterfeit money each year—some of which is produced overseas. Special agents working in a fraud squad often receive complaints or referrals from banking or financial institutions that have been defrauded. Fraud cases involve detailed and long-term investigations to reveal the criminals, who are often organized groups or individuals hiding behind false identifications. Special agents working for forgery squads often have cases referred to them from banks or local police departments that have discovered incidents of forgery.

REQUIREMENTS

High School

You can help prepare for a career as a special agent by doing well in high school. You may receive special consideration by the Secret Service if you have computer training, which is needed to investigate computer fraud, or if you can speak a foreign language, which is useful during investigations and while protecting visiting heads of state or U.S. officials working abroad. Highly regarded are specialized skills in electronics, forensics, and other investigative areas. Aside from school, doing something unique and positive for your city or neighborhood or becoming involved in community organizations can improve your chances of being selected by the Secret Service.

Postsecondary Training

The Secret Service recruits special agents at an entry level GS-5, GS-7, and GS-9 grade levels. You can qualify at the GS-5 level in one of three ways: Obtain a four-year degree from an accredited college or university; work for at least three years in a criminal investigative or law enforcement field and gain knowledge and experience in applying laws relating to criminal violations; or obtain an equivalent combination of education and experience. You can qualify at the GS-7 or GS-9 level by achieving superior academic scores (defined as a grade point average of at least 2.95 on a 4.0 scale), going to graduate school and studying a directly related field, or gaining an additional year of criminal investigative experience.

All newly hired special agents go through 11 weeks of training at the Federal Law Enforcement Training Center in Glynco, Georgia, and then 15 weeks of specialized training at the James J. Rowley Training Center in Beltsville, Maryland. During training, new agents take comprehensive courses in protective techniques, criminal and constitutional law, criminal investigative procedures, use of scientific investigative devices, physical fitness, first aid, the use of firearms, and defensive measures. Special agents also learn about collecting evidence, surveillance techniques, undercover operation, and courtroom demeanor. Specialized training includes skills such as fire fighting and protection aboard airplanes. Classroom study is supplemented by on-the-job training, and special agents go through advanced in-service training throughout their careers.

Newly hired special agents are assigned to one of the Secret Service's many field offices. Their initial work is investigative and is closely supervised. After approximately five years, agents are usually transferred to a protection assignment.

Other Requirements

In addition to fulfilling educational requirements, special agents must meet the following criteria: be a U.S. citizen; be at least 21 and under 37 years of age at the time of appointment; have uncorrected vision no worse than 20/60 in each eye, correctable to 20/20 in each eye; be in excellent health and physical condition; pass the Treasury Enforcement Agent exam; and undergo a complete background investigation, including in-depth interviews, drug screening, medical examination, and polygraph examination.

The Secret Service is looking for smart, upstanding citizens who will give a favorable representation of the U.S. government. "You can be a crackerjack lawyer, but have some ethical problems in your background, and the Service wouldn't hire you as an agent even though it would love to have your expertise," Norm Jarvis says.

Special agents also need dedication, which can be demonstrated through a candidate's grade point average in high school and college. Applicants must have a drug-free background. Even experimental drug use can be a reason to dismiss an applicant from the hiring process. Special agents also need to be confident and honest—with no criminal background.

Since special agents must travel for their jobs, interested applicants should be flexible and willing to be away from home. Jarvis says traveling was one of the drawbacks of the job, often requiring him to leave his wife and two children at a moment's notice.

EXPLORING

The Secret Service offers the Student Temporary Employment Program (STEP) for college students. The program allows students who meet financial eligibility guidelines to earn money and some benefits by working part time, usually in a clerical job for the agency. There are many requirements and application guidelines for this program, so contact the Secret Service's personnel division at 202-406-5800.

The Secret Service offers the Cooperative Education Program as a way for the agency to identify and train highly motivated students for a career as a special agent. Participants of the paid program learn more about the Secret Service and gain on-the-job training, with the possibility of working full time for the Secret Service upon graduation. The two-year work-study program includes classroom training and hands-on training that will prepare students for the following Secret Service careers: accountant; budget analyst; computer specialist; computer research specialist; electronics engineer; intelligence research specialist; management specialist; personnel management specialist; telecommunications specialist; and visual information specialist. Students working toward a bachelor's degree must complete 1,040 hours of study-related work requirements.

To be considered for the program, you must meet the following criteria: be enrolled full-time in an accredited educational program; be enrolled in your school's cooperative education program; maintain a 3.0 grade point average in either undergraduate or graduate studies; be a U.S. citizen; be enrolled in a field of study related to the position you are applying for; pass a drug test; and pass a preliminary background investigation and possibly a polygraph test. Students in the program work part time, which is between 16 and 32 hours a week. They may work full time during holidays and school breaks. They receive some federal benefits, including a pension plan, low-cost life and health insurance, annual and sick leave, holiday pay, awards, and promotions.

You must submit a variety of forms to apply for this program, so contact the Secret Service's personnel division at 202-406-5800 for more information. In addition, you may be able to apply for the program through the cooperative education program at your school.

EMPLOYERS

Secret Service special agents are employed by the U.S. Secret Service, which is part of the Department of Homeland Security. The service employs approximately 3,200 special agents.

STARTING OUT

Jarvis didn't set out to become a special agent. As a teenager, he admired a neighbor who worked as a deputy sheriff. As Norm grew older and had to make decisions about college and work, he realized he wanted to go into law enforcement. At the age of 18, he volunteered to go into the U.S. Army to train with the military police. When Norm left the service, he used his VA benefits to help him get a bachelor's degree in psychology from Westminster College. "I have an innate interest in why people do the things they do," he says. Norm also earned a master's degree in public administration from the University of Utah. He spent eight years working as a police officer before he decided to apply with the Secret Service. He wasn't satisfied with his police officer's salary and was tired of the "day-to-day emotional trauma of being an officer." Norm loved to travel and was impressed by some special agents he had met, so he decided that becoming a special agent would be a way for him to progress professionally and work in an exciting position. He applied for the job and began working as a special agent assigned to Salt Lake City in 1984.

The Secret Service states that the hiring process is extremely competitive. There are many well-qualified applicants for available positions. On top of that, the hiring process can take up to a year—or longer—because of the thoroughness of the selection process. All special-agent candidates must pass a thorough personal interview, the Treasury Enforcement Agent Examination, a physical examination, a polygraph test, drug screening, and an extensive background investigation. The most qualified candidates will then go through in-depth interviews.

If you can make it through the tough screening process and get hired, you'll be employed by the U.S. Secret Service, which is part of the Department of Homeland Security. If you're ready to apply for a special-agent job, make sure you meet the requirements described above. Then submit a typewritten Standard Form 171, Application for Federal Employment. If you went to college, you will also need to submit an official transcript. Alternatively, you can submit an Optional Application for Federal Employment or a resume, but you'll have to complete some accompanying forms, so be sure to check with the Secret Service field office nearest you before doing so to find out exactly what forms to fill out. The field office in your area should be listed in the government section of your telephone book.

To find out what vacancies currently exist with the Secret Service, visit http://www.secretservice.gov.

ADVANCEMENT

Jarvis began working in the Secret Service's Salt Lake City field office in 1984. He was transferred to the Organized Crime Task Force in the Washington, D.C., field office in 1987. In 1990 Norm was promoted to the position of instructor at the Office of Training, and he was transferred to the Presidential Protective Division in 1994. Before retiring, Norm ended up in Montana in 1997 after being promoted to the position of resident agent of the Great Falls office.

Generally, special agents begin their careers by spending five to 10 years performing primarily investigative duties at a field office. Then they are usually assigned to a protective assignment for three to five years. After 10 years, special agents become eligible to move into supervisory positions. A typical promotion path moves special agents to the position of senior agent, then resident agent in charge of a district, assistant to the special agent in charge, then special agent in charge of a field office or senior management at headquarters. Promotion is awarded based upon performance, and since the Secret Service employs many highly skilled professionals, competition for promotion is strong.

Special agents can retire after they have 25 years of service or after they are 50 years old. Special agents must retire by the age of 57.

Some retired agents are hired by corporations to organize the logistics of getting either people or products from one place to another. Others work as bodyguards, private investigators, security consultants, and local law enforcement officials.

EARNINGS

Special agents generally receive law enforcement availability pay on top of their base pay. Agents usually start at the GS-5, GS-7, or GS-9 grade levels, which were $25,195, $31,209, and $38,175 in 2006, respectively, plus Law Enforcement Availability Pay (25 percent of their base salary). (Salaries may be slightly higher in some areas with high costs of living.) Agents automatically advance by two pay grades each year, until they reach the GS-11 level. At that point, agents automatically advance by one pay grade per year until they reach the GS-13 level, which paid $65,832 in 2006. Agents must compete for positions above the GS-13 level. Top officials in the Secret Service are appointed to Senior Executive Service (SES) positions who do not receive the availability pay. Senior Executive Service salaries ranged from $109,808 to 165,200 in 2006.

Benefits for special agents include low-cost health and life insurance; annual and sick leave; paid holidays; and a comprehensive retirement program. In addition, free financial protection is provided to agents and their families in the event of job-related injury or death.

WORK ENVIRONMENT

A Secret Service special agent is assigned to a field office, protective assignment, or one of many Washington, D.C., offices. Agents on investigative assignments may spend much time doing research with the office as base, or they may be out in the field, doing undercover or surveillance work. Protective and investigative assignments can keep a special agent away from home for long periods of time, depending on the situation. Preparations for the president's visits to cities in the United States generally take no more than a week. However, a large event attracting foreign dignitaries, such as the Asian Pacific Conference in the state of Washington, can take months to plan. Special agents at field offices assigned to investigate crimes are called out regularly to serve temporary protective missions. During presidential campaign years, agents typically serve three-week protective assignments, work three weeks back at their field offices, and then start the process over again. Special agents work at least 40 hours a week and often work a minimum of 50 hours each week.

One of the drawbacks of being a special agent is the potential danger involved. A special agent was shot in the stomach in 1981 during an assassination attempt on President Ronald Reagan. Other agents have been killed on the job in helicopter accidents, surveillance assignments, and protective operations, to name a few.

For most agents, however, the benefits outweigh the drawbacks. For Norm Jarvis, the excitement and profound importance of his work gave him great job satisfaction. "There are times when you are involved in world history and you witness history being made, or you are present when historical decisions are being made, and you feel privileged to be a part of making history, albeit you're behind the scenes and never recognized for it," he says. However, according to one of Jarvis's coworkers, the job is not always glamorous and can be "like going out in your backyard in your best suit and standing for three hours."

OUTLOOK

Compared to other federal law enforcement agencies, the Secret Service is small. It employs about 6,400 people, 3,200 of whom are special agents. As a result, the number of agents it hires each year is limited. Individuals with prior experience in law enforcement and advanced degrees will have the best employment prospects.

FOR MORE INFORMATION

Your local Secret Service field office or headquarters office can provide more information on becoming a special agent. To learn about careers, download employment applications, and read frequently asked questions, check out the following Web site:

U.S. Secret Service
Tel: 202-406-5800
http://www.secretservice.gov

Urban and Regional Planners

OVERVIEW

Urban and regional planners assist in the development and redevelopment of a city, metropolitan area, or region. They work to preserve historical buildings, protect the environment, and help manage a community's growth and change. Planners evaluate individual buildings and city blocks and are also involved in the design of new subdivisions, neighborhoods, and even entire towns. There are approximately 32,000 urban and regional planners working in the United States.

HISTORY

Cities have always been planned to some degree. Most cultures, from the ancient Greeks to the Chinese to the Native Americans, made some organized plans for the development of their cities. By the fourth century B.C., theories of urban planning existed in the writings of Plato, Aristotle, and Hippocrates. Their ideas concerning the issues of site selection and orientation were later modified and updated by Vitruvius in his *De architectura,* which appeared after 27 B.C. This work helped create a standardized guide to Roman engineers as they built fortified settlements and cities throughout the vast empire. Largely inspired by Vitruvius, 15th-century Italian theorists compiled enormous amounts of information and ideas on urban planning. They replaced vertical walls with angular fortifications for better protection during times

QUICK FACTS

School Subjects
Business
English
Government

Personal Skills
Communication/ideas
Leadership/management

Work Environment
Primarily indoors
Primarily multiple locations

Minimum Education Level
Bachelor's degree

Salary Range
$34,890 to $63,700 to
$84,820+

Certification or Licensing
Voluntary

Outlook
About as fast as the average

DOT
199

GOE
11.03.02

NOC
2153

O*NET-SOC
19-3051.00

of war. They also widened streets and opened up squares by building new churches, halls, and palaces. Early designs were based on a symmetrical style that quickly became fashionable in many of the more prosperous European cities.

Modern urban planning owes much to the driving force of the industrial revolution. The desire for more sanitary living conditions led to the demolition of slums. Laws were enacted to govern new construction and monitor the condition of old buildings. In 1848, Baron George Eugene Haussmann organized the destruction and replacement of 40 percent of the residential quarters in Paris and created new neighborhood park systems. In England, the 1875 Public Health Act allowed municipalities to regulate new construction, the removal of waste, and newly constructed water and sewer systems.

THE JOB

Urban and regional planners assist in the development or maintenance of carefully designed communities. Working for a government agency or as a consultant, planners are involved in integrating new buildings, houses, sites, and subdivisions into an overall city plan. Their plans must coordinate streets, traffic, public facilities, water and sewage, transportation, safety, and ecological factors such as wildlife habitats, wetlands, and floodplains. Planners are also involved in renovating and preserving historic buildings. They work with a variety of professionals, including architects, artists, computer programmers, engineers, economists, landscape architects, land developers, lawyers, writers, and environmental and other special interest groups.

Chris Wayne works as a redevelopment planner for the city of Omaha, Nebraska. His work involves identifying new project sites—buildings that the planning department wants to redevelop—and going about acquiring the property. Before making a purchase, he hires an appraiser to determine the worth of the building and then makes an offer to the building's owner. If the owner accepts and the building is slated for redevelopment, the city may have to vacate the building. "This involves interviewing the residents," Wayne says, "to determine what's necessary for them to move. We determine what amount they'll be compensated." Various community programs assist in finding new housing or providing tenants with moving funds. Once the property has been vacated, the planning department accepts and reviews proposals from developers. A developer is then offered a contract. When demolition and construction begin,

Wayne's department must monitor the project and make the necessary payments.

Urban and regional planners also work with unused or undeveloped land. They may help design the layout for a proposed building, keeping in mind traffic circulation, parking, and the use of open space. Planners are also responsible for suggesting ways to implement these programs or proposals, considering their costs and how to raise funds for them.

Schools, churches, recreational areas, and residential tracts are studied to determine how they will fit into designs for optimal usefulness and beauty. As with other factors, specifications for the nature and kinds of buildings must be considered. Zoning codes, which regulate the specific use of land and buildings, must be adhered to during construction. Planners need to be knowledgeable of these regulations and other legal matters and communicate them to builders and developers.

Some urban and regional planners teach in colleges and schools of planning, and many do consulting work. Planners today are concerned not only with city codes, but also with environmental problems of water pollution, solid waste disposal, water treatment plants, and public housing.

Planners work in older cities or design new ones. Columbia, Maryland, and Reston, Virginia, both built in the 1960s, are examples of planned communities. Before plans for such communities can be developed, planners must prepare detailed maps and charts showing the proposed use of land for housing, business, and community needs. These studies provide information on the types of industries in the area, the locations of housing developments and businesses, and the plans for providing basic needs such as water, sewage treatment, and transportation. After maps and charts have been analyzed, planners design the layout to present to land developers, city officials, housing experts, architects, and construction firms.

The following short descriptions list the wide variety of planners within the field.

Human services planners develop health and social service programs to upgrade living standards for those lacking opportunities or resources. These planners frequently work for private health care organizations and government agencies.

Historic preservation planners use their knowledge of the law and economics to help preserve historic buildings, sites, and neighborhoods. They are frequently employed by state agencies, local governments, and the National Park Service.

Transportation planners, working mainly for government agencies, oversee the transportation infrastructure of a community, keeping in mind local priorities such as economic development and environmental concerns.

Housing and community development planners analyze housing needs to identify potential opportunities and problems that may affect a neighborhood and its surrounding communities. Such planners are usually employed by private real estate and financial firms, local governments, and community development organizations.

Economic development planners, usually employed by local governments or chambers of commerce, focus on attracting and retaining industry to a specific community. They communicate with industry leaders who select sites for new plants, warehouses, and other major projects.

Environmental planners advocate the integration of environmental issues into building construction, land use, and other community objectives. They work at all levels of government and for some nonprofit organizations.

Urban design planners work to design and locate public facilities, such as churches, libraries, and parks, to best serve the larger community. Employers include large-scale developers, private consulting firms, and local governments.

International development planners specialize in strategies for transportation, rural development, modernization, and urbanization. They are frequently employed by international agencies, such as the United Nations, and by national governments in less developed countries.

REQUIREMENTS

High School

You should take courses in government and social studies to learn about the past and present organizational structure of cities and counties. You need good communication skills for working with people in a variety of professions, so take courses in speech and English composition. Drafting, architecture, and art classes will familiarize you with the basics of design. Become active on your student council so that you can be involved in implementing changes for the school community.

Postsecondary Training

A bachelor's degree is the minimum requirement for most trainee jobs with federal, state, or local government boards and agencies. However, more opportunities for employment and advancement are available to those with a master's degree. Typical courses include geography, public administration, political science, law, engineering, architecture, landscape architecture, real estate, finance, and management. Computer courses and training in statistical techniques are also essential. Most masters' programs last a minimum of two years and require students to participate in internships with city planning departments.

When considering schools, check with the American Planning Association (APA) for a list of accredited undergraduate and graduate planning programs. The APA can also direct you to scholarship and fellowship programs available to students enrolled in planning programs.

Certification or Licensing

Although not a requirement, obtaining certification in urban and regional planning can lead to more challenging, better-paying positions. The American Institute of Certified Planners, a division of the APA, grants certification to planners who meet certain academic and professional requirements and successfully complete an examination. The exam tests for knowledge of the history and future of planning, research methods, plan implementation, and other relevant topics.

Other Requirements

Chris Wayne pursued a master's in urban studies because he was drawn to community development. "I was interested in the social interaction of people and the space they occupy, such as parks and plazas," he says.

In addition to being interested in planning, you should have design skills and a good understanding of spatial relationships. Good analytical skills will help you in evaluating projects. Planners must be able to visualize the relationships between streets, buildings, parks, and other developed spaces and anticipate potential planning problems. As a result, logic and problem-solving abilities are also important.

EXPLORING

Research the origins of your city by visiting your county courthouse and local library. Check out early photographs and maps of your area to give you an idea of what went into the planning of your community. Visit local historic areas to learn about the development and history behind old buildings. You may also

Planning Specializations

- Community Activism/Empowerment
- Community Development
- Economic Development
- Environmental/Natural Resources Planning
- Historic Preservation
- Housing
- Land Use & Code Enforcement
- Parks & Recreation
- Planning Management/Finance
- Transportation Planning
- Urban Design

Source: American Planning Association

consider getting involved in efforts to preserve local buildings and threatened areas.

With the help of a teacher or academic adviser, arrange to interview a working planner to gain details of his or her job. Another good way to see what planners do is to attend a meeting of a local planning commission, which by law is open to the public. Interested students can find out details about upcoming meetings through their local paper or planning office.

EMPLOYERS

There are approximately 32,000 urban and regional planners working in the United States. Seven out of 10 of planners work for local governments; others work for state agencies, the federal government, and in the private sector.

Many planners are hired for full-time work where they intern. Others choose to seek opportunities in state and federal governments and nonprofit organizations. Planners work for government agencies that focus on particular areas of city research and development, such as transportation, the environment, and housing. Urban and regional planners are also sought by colleges, law firms, the

United Nations, and even foreign governments of rapidly modernizing countries.

STARTING OUT

With a bachelor's degree, a beginning worker may start out as an assistant at an architectural firm or construction office. Others start out working as city planning aides in regional or urban offices. New planners research projects, conduct interviews, survey the field, and write reports on their findings. Those with a master's degree can enter the profession at a higher level, working for federal, state, and local agencies.

Previous work experience in a planning office or with an architectural or engineering firm is useful before applying for a job with city, county, or regional planning agencies. Membership in a professional organization is also helpful in locating job opportunities. These include the American Planning Association, the American Institute of Architects, the American Society of Civil Engineers, and the International City/County Management Association. Most of these organizations host student chapters that provide information on internship opportunities and professional publications. (See the end of this article for contact information.)

Because many planning staffs are small, directors are usually eager to fill positions quickly. As a result, job availability can be highly variable. Students are advised to apply for jobs before they complete their degree requirements. Most colleges have career services offices to assist students in finding job leads.

ADVANCEMENT

Beginning assistants can advance within the planning board or department to eventually become planners. The positions of senior planner and planning director are successive steps in some agencies. Frequently, experienced planners advance by moving to a larger city or county planning board, where they become responsible for larger and more complicated projects, make policy decisions, or become responsible for funding new developments. Other planners may become consultants to communities that cannot afford a full-time planner. Some planners also serve as city managers, cabinet secretaries, and presidents of consulting firms.

EARNINGS

Earnings vary based on position, work experience, and the population of the city or town the planner serves. According to the U.S. Department of Labor, median annual earnings of urban and regional planners were $54,590 in 2004. The lowest 10 percent earned less than $34,890, and the highest 10 percent earned more than $84,820. Mean annual earnings in local government, the industry employing the largest numbers of urban and regional planners, were $55,410. According to an American Planning Association survey of its members, the median annual salary for planners was $63,700 in 2006. It also reported that its certified members earned an average of $13,000 more than those who were not certified.

Because many planners work for government agencies, they usually have sick leave and vacation privileges and are covered by retirement and health plans. Many planners also have access to a city-owned automobile.

Planners who work as consultants are generally paid on a fee basis. Their earnings are often high and vary greatly according to their reputations and work experience. Their earnings will depend on the number of consulting jobs they accept.

WORK ENVIRONMENT

Planners spend a considerable amount of time in an office setting. However, in order to gather data about the areas they develop, planners also spend much of their time outdoors examining the surrounding land, structures, and traffic. Most planners work standard 40-hour weeks, but they may also attend evening or weekend council meetings or public forums to share upcoming development proposals.

Planners work alone and with land developers, public officials, civic leaders, and citizens' groups. Occasionally, they may face opposition from interest groups against certain development proposals and, as a result, they must have the patience needed to work with disparate groups. The job can be stressful when trying to keep tight deadlines or when defending proposals in both the public and private sectors.

OUTLOOK

The U.S. Department of Labor expects the overall demand for urban and regional planners to grow about as fast as the average for all occupations through 2014. Communities turn to professional planners for help in meeting demands resulting from urbanization and the growth in population. Urban and regional planners are needed to zone and plan land use for undeveloped and rural areas as well as commercial development in rapidly growing suburban areas. There will be jobs available with non-governmental agencies that deal with historic preservation and redevelopment. Opportunities also exist in maintaining existing bridges, highways, and sewers, and in preserving and restoring historic sites and buildings.

Factors that may affect job growth include government regulation regarding the environment, housing, transportation, and land use. The redevelopment of inner-city areas and the expansion of suburban areas will serve to provide many jobs for planners. However, when communities face budgetary constraints, planning departments may be reduced before others, such as police forces or education.

FOR MORE INFORMATION

For more information on careers, contact
    American Institute of Architects
    1735 New York Avenue, NW
    Washington, DC 20006-5292
    Tel: 800-242-3837
    Email: infocentral@aia.org
    http://www.aia.org

For more information on careers, certification, and accredited planning programs, contact
    American Planning Association
    122 South Michigan Avenue, Suite 1600
    Chicago, IL 60603-6147
    Tel: 312-431-9100
    Email: CareerInfo@planning.org http://www.planning.org

For career guidance and information on student chapters as well as a list of colleges that offer civil engineering programs, contact
    American Society of Civil Engineers
    1801 Alexander Bell Drive
    Reston, VA 20191-4400
    Tel: 800-548-2723
    http://www.asce.org

To learn about city management and the issues affecting today's cities, visit this Web site or contact

International City/County Management Association
777 North Capitol Street, NE, Suite 500
Washington, DC 20002-4290
Tel: 202-289-4262
http://www.icma.org

Index

A

Adams, John 5
admeasurers 97
administrative assistants 16, 24
agricultural chemical inspectors 95
agricultural-chemical registration specialists 95
agricultural commodity graders 95
agricultural quarantine inspectors 95
agricultural specialist 33
Agriculture, U.S. Department of 104
Air Force Recruiting Service Headquarters, U.S. 152
air marshals 70–71
alcohol, tobacco, and firearms inspectors 98
ambassadors 5–13
  advancement 11
  earnings 11
  employers 9
  exploring 9
  high school requirements 7
  history 5–6
  job, described 6–7
  outlook 12
  overview 5
  postsecondary training 8
  requirements 7–9
  starting out 9–11
  work environment 11–12
American Bar Association (ABA) 131
American Foreign Service Association 12, 91
American Institute of Architects 193
American Literary Translators Association 123–124
American Planning Association 193
American Postal Workers Union 141
American Society of Civil Engineers 193
American Translators Association 124
archaeologists 154

Aristotle 60, 185
Armed Forces Vocational Aptitude Battery 145
Army Recruiting Command Headquarters, U.S. 152
Arnold, Benedict 105–106
assistant city managers 16
Association of American Law Schools 131
Association of Former Intelligence Officers 112–113
attendance officers 96
automobile testers 97
aviation safety inspectors 97
aviation security director 71

B

baggage and passenger screener 70
bank examiners 98
Begich, Mark 172–173
Border Patrol. *See* Customs and Border Protection, U.S. Bureau of
Bush, George W. 106, 144

C

canine enforcement officers 35
case officers 107
caseworkers 25
Catherine II (empress of Russia) 6
Central Intelligence Agency (CIA) 113
chemist 35–36
chief executive 166
chief of staff, congressional 24
Citizenship and Immigration Services, Bureau of U.S. 103
city managers 14–21, 167
  advancement 19
  earnings 19
  employers 18
  exploring 17–18
  high school requirements 16
  history 14
  job, described 15–16
  outlook 20
  overview 14

postsecondary training 16–17
requirements 16–17
starting out 18–19
work environment 20
Clinton, Bill 174
Coast Guard Recruiting, U.S. 152
commercial officers 85
commissioners 167
Computer Investigations and
Infrastructure Threat Assessment
Center 49–50
computer operators 25
conference interpreters 116
congressional aides 22–30
advancement 27
Congressional Management
Foundation 29
earnings 28
employers 26–27
exploring 26
high school requirements 25
history 22–23
job, described 23–25
outlook 29
overview 22
work environment 28
Congressional Management
Foundation 67
consular officers foreign service officers 85
council members 166–167
Council of State Governments 68
counterintelligence agents 108
county clerk 167
county treasurer 167
court interpreters 114, 116
criminal investigators 36
cryptographic technicians 107
cultural officers foreign service officers 86
custom pilots 35
Customs and Border Protection, U.S.
Bureau of 32, 33, 35–36, 39
customs inspectors 96–97
customs officials 31–39
advancement 38
earnings 38
employers 37
exploring 37
high school requirements 36

history 32
job, described 32–36
outlook 39
overview 31
postsecondary training 36–37
requirements 36–37
starting out 38
work environment 38–39

D

Dana, Francis 5, 6
deaf, interpreters for 114
Defense Intelligence Agency 113
Department of... See under specific
departments, e.g.: Agriculture, U.S.
Department of
deputy U.S. marshals 40–47
advancement 45–46
earnings 46
employers 45
exploring 45
high school requirements 44
history 40–41
job, described 41–43
outlook 47
overview 40
postsecondary training 44
requirements 44–45
starting out 45
work environment 46–47

E

Earp, Wyatt 41
economic development planners
188
economic officers 85
enforcement rangers 154
enlisted personnel 145
environmental health inspectors 95
environmental planners 188
Environmental Protection Agency,
U.S. 104
escort interpreters 116
executive assistants 16

F

FBI (Federal Bureau of Investigation)
57, 113
FBI Academy 52–53

FBI agents **48–59**
  advancement 55–56
  earnings 56
  employers 55
  exploring 53–55
  high school requirements 51
  history 48–50
  job, described 50–51
  outlook 57
  overview 48
  postsecondary training 51–53
  requirements 51–53
  Ross Rice interview 57–59
  starting out 55
  work environment 56–57
FBI Honors Internship Program
  53–54, 110
federal and state officials **60–68**
  advancement 66
  earnings 66
  employers 65
  exploring 64–65
  high school requirements 62–63
  history 60–61
  job, described 61–62
  outlook 67
  overview 60
  postsecondary training 63
  requirements 62–64
  starting out 65
  work environment 66–67
Federal Aviation Administration
  (FAA) 75
federal aviation security worker
  69–75
  advancement 74
  earnings 74
  employers 73
  exploring 72–73
  high school requirements 71
  history 69–70
  job, described 70–71
  outlook 74–75
  overview 69
  postsecondary training 71–72
  requirements 71–72
  starting out 73
  work environment 74
Federal Bar Association (FBA)
  131

Federal Bureau of Investigation.
  See FBI (Federal Bureau of
  Investigation)
Federal Judicial Center 132
Federal Law Enforcement Training
  Center 178–179
Federal Rules of Criminal Procedure
  52
fish and game wardens **76–82**
  advancement 81
  earnings 81
  employers 80
  exploring 80
  high school requirements 78–79
  history 76–77
  job, described 77–78
  outlook 82
  overview 76
  postsecondary training 79
  requirements 78–80
  starting out 80–81
  work environment 81–82
Fish and Wildlife Service, U.S. 82
food and drug inspectors 94
foreign service officers **83–92**
  advancement 89–90
  earnings 90
  employers 88
  exploring 88
  high school requirements 86
  history 83–84
  job, described 84–86
  outlook 91
  overview 83
  postsecondary training 86–87
  requirements 86–87
  starting out 88–89
  work environment 90–91
Foreign Service, U.S. 13
Franklin, Benjamin 5, 133

G

government property inspectors 98
Grant, Ulysses S. 153
guide interpreters 116

H

Haussmann, Baron George Eugene
  186

Health and Human Services, U.S.
 Department of 104
health and regulatory inspectors
 93–104
  advancement 101
  certification/licensing 99–100
  earnings 101
  employers 100
  exploring 100
  high school requirements 99
  history 93–94
  job, described 94–99
  outlook 103
  overview 93
  postsecondary training 99
  requirements 99–100
  starting out 101
  work environment 102–103
health inspectors 96
Hippocrates 185
historians 154
historic preservation planners 187
Homeland Security, U.S. Department
 of 113
Hoover, J. Edgar 48–49
House of Representatives, U.S.
 29–30, 68. See also congressional
 aides
housing and community development
 planners 188
human services planners 187
Hussein, Saddam 144

I
Identification Division (FBI) 49
immigration inspectors 96
import specialists 35
information officers 86
inspectors. See specific inspectors,
 e.g.: agricultural chemical
 inspectors
Intelligence Careers.com 113
intelligence officers 105–113
  advancement 111
  earnings 111
  employers 110
  exploring 110
  high school requirements 109
  history 105–106
  job, described 106–109

  outlook 112
  overview 105
  postsecondary training 109
  requirements 109
  starting out 110–111
  work environment 111–112
International City/County
 Management Association 21, 172,
 194
international development planners
 188
interpreters and translators
 114–124
  advancement 120–121
  certification/licensing 117–118
  earnings 121–122
  employers 119–120
  exploring 119
  high school requirements
   116–117
  history 114–115
  job, described 115–116
  outlook 122–123
  overview 114
  postsecondary training 117
  requirements 116–119
  starting out 120
  work environment 122

J
Jarvis, Norm 176–177, 180–181,
 183
Jay, John 5
Jefferson, Thomas 6, 83
judges 125–132
  advancement 130
  certification/licensing 128
  earnings 130
  employers 130
  exploring 129
  high school requirements 127
  history 125–126
  job, described 127
  outlook 131
  overview 125
  postsecondary training 127–128
  requirements 127–129
  starting out 130
  work environment 130–131
judiciary interpreters 114

L

laboratory specialists 51
Laird, Don 134
land acquisition professionals 155
language specialists 51
lead advance agent 175
Lee, Barbara 23, 27
legislative assistants 24
legislative correspondents 24
legislative director 24
license inspectors 99
localization translators 116
logging-operations inspectors 98

M

mail carriers **133–141**
    advancement 138–139
    certification/licensing 136
    earnings 139
    employers 138
    exploring 137–138
    high school requirements 136
    history 133–134
    job, described 134–136
    outlook 140–141
    overview 133
    requirements 136–137
    starting out 138
    work environment 139–140
mailroom managers (congressional aides) 24
maintenance workers 154
management analysts 16
management officers 84
Marine Corps Recruiting Command, U.S. 152
Marshals Service, U.S. 47
marshals, air 70–71
marshals, U.S. *See* deputy U.S. marshals
Masterson, Bat 41
mayors 167
McKinley, William 174
medical interpreters 114
Military Career Guide Online (Web site) 152
Military City (Web site) 152
military workers **142–152**
    advancement 150
    certification/licensing 148

earnings 150–151
employers 149
exploring 149
high school requirements 146–147
history 142–144
job, described 144–146
outlook 151–152
overview 142
postsecondary training 147–148
requirements 146–149
work environment 151
Miller, Diane 162–164
Miller, Judie 78, 79
mine safety and health inspectors 97
motor vehicle inspectors 97
museum curators/directors 156

N

Napoleon Bonaparte 125
National Association for Law Placement 132
National Association of Counties 172
National Association of Judiciary Interpreters and Translators 124
National Association of Letter Carriers, AFL-CIO 141
National Association of Schools of Public Affairs and Administration 21
National Center for State Courts 132
National Conference of State Legislatures 68
National Conservation Training Center 79
National Governors Association 68
National Judicial College 132
National League of Cities 21
National Park Service employees **153–164**
    advancement 159–160
    Diane Miller interview 162–164
    earnings 160
    employers 158–159
    exploring 158
    high school requirements 156–157
    history 153–154
    job, described 154–156
    outlook 161

overview 153
postsecondary training 157
requirements 156–158
starting out 159
work environment 160–161
National Parks Conservation
Association 161
National Park Service, U.S. 82, 162
National Postal Mail Handlers Union
141
National Recreation and Park
Association 161
National Security Agency 113
Navy Recruiting Command. U.S.
152
Newsome, John 23, 27

O

Occupational Safety and Health
Administration 104
occupational safety and health
inspectors 97
office managers 24
officers, military 145

P

page 26
parcel post carriers 135
park planners 156
park police officers 155
park rangers 154
Park Service. *See* National Park
Service, U.S.
park superintendent 156
passport-application examiners 96
personal secretaries 24
personnel officers 84–85
Plato 185
political officers 85–86
postal inspectors 98–99
Postal Service, U.S. 141
postsecondary training 25
press secretaries 24
Prosser, James 84, 87, 89, 91
public diplomacy officers 86

Q

quality control inspectors and coordinators 98

R

railroad inspectors 97
rangers, interpretive 154–155
Reagan, Ronald 106, 183
refuge ranger 78
regional and local officials **165–173**
advancement 169–170
earnings 170
employers 169
exploring 168–169
high school requirements 167
history 165–166
job, described 166–167
Mark Begich interview 172–173
outlook 171–172
overview 165
postsecondary training 167–168
requirements 167–168
starting out 169
work environment 170
Registry of Interpreters for the Deaf
124
regulatory inspectors 96
requirements 25–26
resource managers 156
revenue officers health and regulatory
inspectors 98
Rice, Ross 57–59

S

safety health inspectors 97
sanitarians 95
schedulers 25
scientists 154
Secret Service special agents
174–184
advancement 181–182
earnings 182
employers 180
exploring 179–180
high school requirements 178
history 174–175
job, described 175–178
outlook 183
overview 174
postsecondary training 178–179
requirements 178–179
starting out 180–181
work environment 182–183

Secret Service, U.S. 184
securities compliance examiners 98
security screener 70
Senate, U.S. 29, 68
Senate Placement Office 30
sight translator 114
sign language interpreters 114
Spears, Carol 155
special agents 36, 77–78
Special Operations Group 43
starting out 27
State, U.S. Department of 92
state and district directors 25
strategic intelligence agents 107–108
Student Conservation Association
  161–162
substitute carriers 135–136
Sun-Tzu 105
supervisor, mail carrier 135
Supreme Court of the United States
  132

T

tactical intelligence agents 108
technical analysts 107
Translators and Interpreters Guild
  124
transportation inspectors 97
transportation planners 188
Transportation Security
  Administration 75
truant officers 96

U

Uniform Certified Accountant
  Examination 52

uniformed guard force 155
United States/U.S. Department of.
  See under specific departments, e.g.:
  Agriculture, U.S. Department of
urban and regional planners
  185–194
  advancement 191
  certification/licensing 189
  earnings 192
  employers 190–191
  exploring 189–190
  high school requirements 188
  history 185–186
  job, described 186–188
  outlook 192–193
  overview 185
  postsecondary training
188–189
  requirements 188–189
  starting out 191
  work environment 192
urban design planners 188
USAJOBS 162

V

Vitruvius 185

W

wage-hour compliance inspectors
  98
warrant officers 145
Washington, George 6, 83, 142
Wayne, Chris 186–187
wildlife inspectors 77
Wilson, Woodrow 153